Principles of
Concurrent and
Distributed Programming

Prentice Hall International Series in Computer Science

C. A. R. Hoare, Series Editor

Principles of Concurrent and Distributed Programming

M. BEN-ARI
Technion – Israel Institute of Technology

PRENTICE HALL
New York London Toronto Sydney Tokyo Singapore

Pearson Education Limited
Edinburgh Gate
Harlow
Essex CM20 2JE
England

and Associated Companies throughout the world

Visit us on the World Wide Web at:
http://www.pearsoneduc.com

© Prentice Hall Europe, 1990

Library of Congress Cataloguing-in-Publication Data

Ben-Ari, 1948-
      Principles of concurrent and distributed programming / M. Ben-Ari.
          p.   cm.- (Prentice Hall international series in computer
science)
      Inculeds bibliographical reference.
      ISBN 0-13-711821-X
      1.   Parallel processing (Electronic computers) 2. Electronic data
Processing-Distrbuted processing. I. Title II. Series.
      QA 76.5.B393 1990
      004'.36-dc20   89-39815
                                                                              CIP

British Library Cataloguing in Publication Data

Ben- Ari, M., *1948-*
      Principles of concurrent and distributed programming.-
      (Prentice Hall international series in computer science)
      1.   Computer systems. Operating systems. Concurrent
      I.   Title.
      005.4'2

      ISBN 0-13-711821-X

10 9 8 7 6 5 4
05 04 03 02 01

Contents

Preface

The field of concurrent programming has seen an explosive expansion since the publication of my previous book *Principles of Concurrent Programming*. Two factors have dictated the need for an entirely new text: the increasing importance of distributed computing and the routine use in industry of languages containing primitives for concurrency such as Ada and occam. The aim of the book remains unchanged: it is an introductory textbook on concurrent programming that focuses on general principles and not on specific systems. The student who masters the material will be prepared not only to read the research literature, but also to evaluate systems, algorithms and languages from a broad perspective.

The intended audience includes advanced undergraduate and beginning graduate students, as well as practicing software engineers interested in obtaining a scientific background in this field. The book assumes a high level of 'computer maturity', such as would be achieved by 2–3 years of a computer science major or practical experience. At the very least, courses in data structures, programming languages and computer architecture should be required prerequisites.

The scope of the material has been limited to concurrent execution of processes, excluding the very low-grained concurrency of large parallel computers and at the other extreme the very high-grained concurrency of computer networks. Within this scope, the choice of material has been guided by pedagogical considerations. An algorithm, language or system is described because it demonstrates some fundamental concept or unusual behavior. Pointers to the current state of the art are given in the references.

The book is divided into three parts and a set of appendices. Part I covers classical concurrent programming similar to the treatment in *Principles of Concurrent Programming*, though there is more use of formal notation. Part II covers distributed programming. Three very different languages are described and compared: Ada, occam and Linda. This is followed by several chapters on distributed algorithms. Part III discusses *principles* of the the implementation of concurrency. A unique feature is the treatment of concurrent programming in real-time systems.

The Ada programming language is used uniformly throughout the book. Ada is probably the only language with embedded concurrent primitives for which high-quality implementations are available on a wide range of computers from mainframes through workstations and down to personal computers. The appendices provide an overview of Ada, as well as code to emulate other primitives (semaphores, monitors, occam, Linda) in Ada.

The program fragments in the text have been expanded into complete executable Ada programs. The source code is available on diskette. Also on the diskette is a very simple concurrency simulator called AdaS written in Turbo Pascal for a personal computer. AdaS can be used to demonstrate the pathological behavior of the examples in Chapter 3 which a true Ada compiler may not be able to show because it does not let the user precisely control the scheduler.

When teaching a course, the instructor can choose from three different types of exercises:

1. Solving the theoretical questions appended to the chapters in Parts I and II.

2. Experimenting with the Ada examples and with AdaS.

3. Writing a concurrent program. A list of suggested problems is given in Section 1.6.

The book was written during a sabbatical year at Brandeis University. I would like to thank the faculty and staff of the university for their support and encouragement. I would also like to thank the Digital Equipment Corporation for the loan of their Ada compiler. Finally, I am indebted to my students both at the Technion and at Brandeis for their patience with me during my experiments with the choice of material and the form of presentation.

M. Ben-Ari
Haifa, 1989

Credits

The following figures have been reprinted or adapted by permission:

- Figure 9.4 from [JG88]. ©Prentice Hall International.
- Figures 13.2–13.5 from [LSP82]. ©ACM.
- Figures 15.4–15.5 from [In85]. ©Inmos.
- Figure 15.8 from [ACG86]. ©IEEE.
- Figure 16.9 from [LL73]. ©ACM.

Trademarks

- Inmos and occam of Inmos, Ltd.
- VAX and VMS of Digital Equipment Corporation.
- Turbo Pascal of Borland International, Inc.
- Alsys of Alsys, Inc.

PART I

Concurrent Programming

Chapter 1

What is Concurrent Programming?

1.1   Introduction

An 'ordinary' program consists of data declarations and executable instructions in a programming language. The instructions are executed *sequentially* on a computer which also allocates memory to hold the data. A *concurrent program* is a set of ordinary sequential programs which are executed in *abstract* parallelism. We use the word *process* for the sequential programs and save the term *program* for the set of processes.

The parallelism is abstract because we do not require that a separate physical *processor* be used to execute each process. Even if the concurrent program is executed by sharing the power of one processor, we can better understand the program by pretending that each process is being executed in parallel. Conversely, even if the processes are actually executed simultaneously on several processors, the mathematical treatment is simplified if we impose an order on the instructions that is compatible with shared execution on a single processor. Like any abstraction, concurrent programming is important because the behavior of wide range of real systems can be modeled and studied without unnecessary detail.

In this book we will define formal models of concurrent programs and study algorithms written in these formalisms. Because of the possible interactions among the processes that comprise a concurrent program, it is exceedingly difficult to write a correct program for even the simplest problem. New tools are needed to specify, program and verify these programs. Unless these are understood, a programmer used to writing and testing sequential programs may be totally mystified by the bizarre behavior that a concurrent program can exhibit.

Despite our commitment to abstraction, concurrent programming arose from problems encountered in creating real systems. To motivate the abstraction, we now present a series of real-world examples of concurrency.

1.2   Overlapped I/O and Computation

It is difficult to grasp intuitively the speed of electronic devices. The fingers of a 60 words-per-minute typist seem to fly across the keyboard, to say nothing of the

3

impression of speed given by a 200 characters-per-second printer. Yet these rates are extremely slow compared with the time required by the computer to process each character which may be about 10 microseconds.

Let us multiply the time scale by one million so that every microsecond becomes a second. Then every second becomes 11.5 days. If you were a computer, processing the characters being typed in, you would have to do 10 seconds of work every 2.3 days. Even if you had to process characters being sent to the printer, it would require only 10 seconds of work every 1.4 hours – hardly a strenuous job.

The tremendous gap between the speeds of human and mechanical processing on the one hand, and the speed of electronic devices on the other led to the development of operating systems which allow I/O operations to proceed 'in parallel' with computation. Obviously, controlling I/O (getting a character from the keyboard and placing it in memory) cannot be done in parallel with other computation on a single computer, but it is possible to 'steal' the few microseconds needed to control the I/O from the main computation. As can be seen from the numbers in the previous paragraph, the degradation in performance will not be noticeable, even when the overhead of switching is included.

What is the connection between overlapped I/O and concurrency? It would be theoretically possible for every program to include code that would periodically sample the keyboard and the printer to see if they need to be serviced. Alternatively, an I/O device could be instructed to cause the processor to jump to a pre-defined place in the program whenever it needs processing. However, these techniques require that every programmer include code to control every I/O device on the computer.

It is conceptually simpler to program the I/O controllers as separate *processes* which are executed in parallel with the main computation process (Figure 1.1). Of course we all know that on a single processor, the processes will not be executed in parallel, but the concurrent programming abstraction allows us to write independent programs for each device and free the application programmer from the details of the system. The techniques described in this book show how to *synchronize* the execution of the processes and how to *communicate* data among them.

1.3 Multi-programming

It is not too difficult to construct an operating system that overlaps I/O and computation. It is more difficult to write an applications program that takes advantage of this. Most programs are written to loop through a cycle: `Read`; `Process`; `Write` and it is not easy to design a program that correctly manages the data structures needed for concurrent I/O.

A simple generalization of the overlapped I/O within a single program is to overlap the computation and I/O of several programs (Figure 1.2). Each program can execute a simple `Read`; `Process`; `Write` cycle and the I/O of one is overlapped with the computation of another. *Multi-programming* is the concurrent execution of several independent programs on one processor.

An additional generalization is *time-slicing* – sharing the processor among

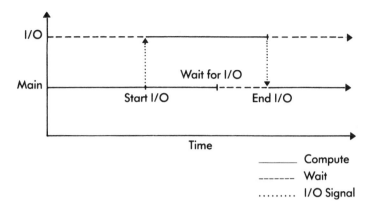

Figure 1.1 Overlapped I/O and computation

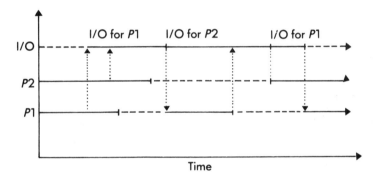

Figure 1.2 Multi-programming

several computations. Rather than wait for a computation to block pending completion of an I/O operation, a (hardware) timer is used to interrupt a computation at pre-determined intervals, for example every half second. A *scheduler* program is run by the operating system to determine which process should be allowed to run for the next interval. The scheduler can take into account priority considerations.

Interactive time-sharing systems use time-sliced multi-programming to give a group of users the illusion that each one has access to a dedicated computer. Of course, the computer will have to be much more powerful than one that could support only a single user so that the *response time* to a request remains acceptable. The fluctuation in the computing requirements of a group of users allows a time-sharing system to give good service while achieving economies of scale. Of course, if the system is overloaded with too many users, the response times will become unacceptable. A further advantage of a time-sharing system is that large computations can be run at a low priority to 'soak up' unused computing power and they can run during periods of light use such as nights and weekends.

Multi-programming can even be useful on a personal computer or workstation where all the work is being done for one user. In a typical configuration, several processes will be concurrently active, each with its own *window* on the screen for interaction with the user (Figure 1.3). These are:

- A background calculation on a spreadsheet.
- A word processor for writing a memo.
- A communications program receiving mail from a network.

The key to the successful use of multi-programming in a single-user environment is to ensure that concurrently active programs use different resources: the processor, the disk, the display, etc. If we had two processes using the processor intensively, we would pay for the overhead of concurrency and experience degraded performance with no apparent advantage.

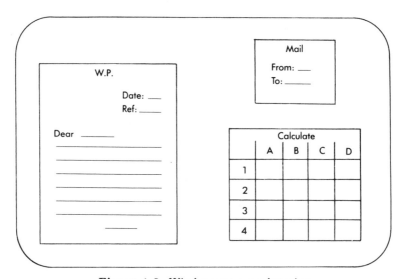

Figure 1.3 Windows on a workstation

Clearly, the concurrent programming abstraction is applicable to multi-programming. We cannot build one program that computes what every user wants. We can let each user write a program and run them in abstract parallelism by sharing a single computer.

1.4   Multi-tasking

Further generalization leads to *multi-tasking*: solving a problem by decomposition into several concurrent processes. When this is done careful attention must be paid to the *grain* of concurrency: how small are the tasks going to be? The smaller the tasks, the more potential concurrency but the higher the overhead.

Small-grained concurrency requires hardware support to be efficient. A simple example is a computer with separate processors for multiplication and addition. In Figure 1.4, **A*B** and **C+D** can be done in parallel, followed by the second addition. An *array* processor is able to perform a single operation on all elements of an array in parallel (Figure 1.5). While small-grained concurrency can be modeled with the help of the abstractions described in this book, ultimately it is closely connected with specific machine architectures and specific application problems and is better studied in those frameworks. Thus we turn our attention to large-grained concurrency.

```
E := (A*B) + (C+D);
```

Figure 1.4 Parallel function units

```
for I in 1..100 loop
  A(I) := B(I) + C(I)*D(I);
end loop;
```

Figure 1.5 Parallel vector processing

At the other extreme is concurrency on the level of independent programs. Multi-programming operating systems are an obvious example. The Unix operating system provides a convenient mechanism for running programs concurrently. The output of one program may be directly connected to the input of another via a *pipe* (Figure 1.6). The operating system causes an output buffer of one program to be passed as an input buffer of the next program, rather than having the data written to disk and read back in. Not only does this avoid unnecessary disk access, but also it enables programs to be run incrementally making it possible to examine the output as the programs are running.

```
sort | remove_duplicates | format | print
```

Figure 1.6 Pipes in Unix

The typical problem we have in mind for large-grained concurrent programming is one which is divided into a 'few' processes which co-operate to solve the problem, or one where several processes compete for resources. *Real-time embedded* systems are an important class of systems that are constructed using multi-tasking. These are computers that are part of larger systems: aircraft, radar installations, X-ray scanners, power plants. They are required to sample environmental inputs, do calculations and control outputs all within strict requirements on response times that can be as short as several milliseconds. A real-time system is constructed as a set of processes which are scheduled to meet the timing constraints. Constructing real-time systems is particularly challenging because existing formalisms do not adequately cover absolute timing requirements. Nevertheless, the languages and algorithms of concurrent programming are the tools used to create real-time systems.

Finally, it can be useful to decompose an ordinary sequential program into a multi-tasking program. Multi-tasking can simplify the solution of a problem and it can be used to improve performance on a *multi-processor* – a computer with several processors, or a *multi-computer* – a system with several complete computers connected together.

Consider the outline of a word-processor:

- Read characters and collect as words.
- Collect words to fill a line.
- Hyphenate, if necessary.
- Introduce spaces to justify the line with the right margin.
- Collect enough lines to make a page.
- Print the page.

This is an 'ordinary' program that can be sequentially executed from start to finish. Nevertheless, it is not easy to program sequentially. For example, hyphenation may require a portion of a word to be 'returned' to the stream of words to await the next line. The program will be much easier to understand if it is written as a set of concurrent processes even if it is to be run sequentially.

An example of performance improvement is the Mergesort algorithm (Figure 1.7). As a sequential algorithm, we sort each half of the array and then merge the results. If we have a multi-processor, the two sorts can be done in true parallelism to improve performance. For example, if the input sequence is $(4, 2, 7, 6, 1, 8, 5, 0, 3, 9)$, the two Sort procedures can be run in parallel on $(4, 2, 7, 6, 1)$ and $(8, 5, 0, 3, 9)$ to give $(1, 2, 4, 6, 7)$ and $(0, 3, 5, 8, 9)$, respectively. Merge combines these to give the final result: $(0, 1, 2, 3, 4, 5, 6, 7, 8, 9)$. We need a concurrent programming language to express the fact that the two calls to Sort can be done in parallel and to ensure that Merge commences only after they have both terminated.

```
procedure Merge_Sort is
   A: array(1..N) of Integer;
   procedure Sort(Low, High: Integer);
   procedure Merge;
begin
   Sort(1,     N/2);
   Sort(N/2+1, N);
   Merge;
end;
```

Figure 1.7 Mergesort

Actually, there is more potential parallelism in this algorithm. If Sort produces its output incrementally in ascending order, Merge can also be run in parallel. The partial results $(1, 2)$ and $(0, 3)$ can be merged to obtain a partial answer $(0, 1, 2)$ without waiting for the rest of the data. To implement this parallelism will require synchronization and communication. Each merge step must be synchronized with the production of a new result from one of the sorts and these results must be communicated from Sort to Merge. Concurrent programming structures can express the required parallelism and provide programming instructions for synchronization and communication.

1.5 An Outline of the Book

The book is divided into three parts. The first deals with concurrent programming in *common-memory* architectures. These are computers in which processes share access to memory locations or are able to call a centralized operating system to receive a service. Common-memory algorithms are appropriate for concurrent programs that execute by sharing a single computer. They may also be appropriate for multi-processor architectures that have shared memory.

Chapter 2 describes the abstraction that is used (interleaved execution sequences of atomic instructions), defines what it means for a concurrent program to be correct and introduces the methods used to prove correctness. The simplest atomic instruction is a single access to a memory location. Chapter 3 develops algorithms for this model. The chapter is central because it demonstrates in full detail the possible pathological behaviors that a concurrent program can exhibit, as well as verification techniques that can be used to prove correctness.

Chapters 4 and 5 treat the classic concurrent programming primitives, the semaphore and the monitor, that are implemented in terms of an underlying operating system. The ideas are reinforced in Chapter 6 where the problem of the dining philosophers is solved.

Part II deals with *distributed systems* which communicate by exchanging messages. They are intended to model systems where processes execute on physically separated processors.

After an introductory chapter (7) defining the models, three languages are presented in Chapters 8–10: *Ada*, *occam* and *Linda*. These languages are all intended for distributed systems, but their designers chose radically different primitives for expressing concurrency. Comparing the languages gives a broad perspective on the field of distributed computation.

Chapters 11–13 describe three algorithms for distributed systems:

Mutual exclusion The distributed version of the problem studied in Chapter 3.

Termination How can a set of distributed processes agree that a global state exists?

Byzantine Generals An introduction to the subject of fault-tolerance in distributed systems.

Part III discusses the implementation of concurrent programs. Chapter 14 describes the implementation of concurrent programming on a single processor computer. This gives an overview of some of the topics usually taught in a course on 'operating systems'. Chapter 15 presents some examples of the implementation of the three distributed languages: Ada, occam and Linda. Finally, Chapter 16 studies real-time systems where concurrent programming techniques may need modification to ensure correctness under constraints on response time.

The examples are written in the Ada programming language. They use as little of the language as is necessary to demonstrate concurrent programming. In particular, the complex type system is not employed. Appendix A briefly describes the features of the language that are used so that the reader unacquainted with Ada will be able to follow the examples.

Appendix B explains how to convert the fragmentary examples in the text into executable Ada programs. It also describes an implementation of semaphores and monitors in Ada.

Appendix C contains an emulation of the occam and Linda concurrent programming primitives in Ada. Finally, Appendix D describes an implementation of distributed algorithms of Part III.

1.6   Concurrent Programming Problems

The problems in this section can be used as programming exercises. Following each problem is either a reference to the chapter where the problem is discussed, or the outline of one or more solutions. The solutions differ in the amount of concurrency in the program. In a real system, a solution should be chosen that matches the parallelism in the computer and the available synchronization primitives.

1. Mergesort (this chapter).

2. Bounded buffer (Chapter 4).

3. Readers and writers (Chapter 5).

4. Dining philosophers (Chapter 6).

5. Matrix multiplication (Chapter 9, 10).

6. The sum of a set of N numbers.

    *   Solution 1: Two processes each compute the sum of $N/2$ numbers from the set. A third process receives the two sums and computes the final answer.

    *   Solution 2: Create a binary tree of processes of depth d. This tree has 2^d leaves, each of which computes the sum of $N/2^d$ numbers and passes the partial results to its parent. An interior process adds the values passed to it by its sons. The output of the root process is the final answer.

    *   Solution 3: A set of k processes each has access to the entire set of numbers. A process removes two numbers, adds them and returns the result to the set. When there is only one number in the set, the program terminates and returns that value.

7. (Conway) The program reads 80-character records and writes the data as records of 125 characters. An extra blank is appended after each input record and every pair of asterisks (**) is replaced by an exclamation point (!).

    *   Solution: Use three processes, one to read and decompose the input records, one to filter the asterisk pairs and one to compose the output records.

8. (Manna and Pnueli) Compute the binomial coefficient:

$$(n\ k) = n(n-1)\ldots(n-k+1)/1 \times 2\ldots k$$

- Solution 1: One process computes the numerator and a second process computes the denominator. A third process does the division.

- Solution 2: Note (prove) that $i!$ divides $j(j+1)\ldots(j+i-1)$. The numerator process can receive partial results from the denominator process and do the division immediately, keeping the intermediate results from becoming too big. For example, 1×2 divides 10×9, $1 \times 2 \times 3$ divides $10 \times 9 \times 8$, and so on.

9. (Roussel) Given two binary trees with labeled leaves, check if the sequence of labels is the same in each tree. For example, the two trees defined by the expressions $(a, (b, c))$ and $((a, b), c)$ have the same sequence of leaves.

- Solution: Create two processes to traverse the trees concurrently. They will send the leaf labels in the order encountered to a third process for comparison.

10. (Dijkstra) Let S and T be two disjoint sets of numbers where s and t are the number of elements in the sets. Write a program which modifies the two sets so that S contains the s smallest members of $S \cup T$ and T contains the t largest members of $S \cup T$.

- Solution 1: Process Ps finds the largest element in S and sends it to Pt which then finds the smallest element in T and sends it to Ps. What is the termination condition?

- Solution 2: Create $S \cup T$. Let process Ps extract the s smallest elements and Pt extract the t largest elements.

11. (Conway) The game of Life. A set of cells is arranged in a (potentially infinite) rectangular array so that each cell has eight neighbors (horizontally, vertically and diagonally). Each cell is 'alive' or 'dead'. Given an initial finite set of 'alive' cells, compute the configuration obtained after a sequence of generations. The rules for passing from one generation to the next are:

(a) If a cell is alive and has less than two live neighbors, it dies.

(b) If it has two or three live neighbors, it continues to live.

(c) If it has four or more live neighbors, it dies.

(d) A dead cell with exactly three live neighbors becomes alive.

- Solution: Each cell is simulated by a process. There are two problems to be solved. Firstly, the computation of the next generation must be synchronized, i.e. the modification of every cell must be based on the status of neighboring cells in the same generation. Secondly, a large data structure of processes and communications channels must be created.

12. (Hoare) Write a disk server that minimizes the amount of seek time done by the arm of a disk drive. A simple server could satisfy requests for data in decreasing order of distance from the current position of the arm. Unfortunately, this could starve a request for data if closer requests arrive too fast.

   - Solution: Maintain two queues of requests: one for requests for data from track numbers less than the current position and one for requests with higher track numbers. Satisfy all requests from one queue before considering requests from the other queue. Make sure that a stream of requests for data from the current track cannot cause starvation.

13. Compute all prime numbers from 2 to n. Note (prove) that if k is not a prime, it is divisible by a prime $p(k) \leq \sqrt{k} + 1$.

   - Solution 1: Allocate a process for each number k from 2 to n. Check if k is divisible by any number less than or equal to $\sqrt{k} + 1$.

   - Solution 2: Allocate processes for each k and have them delete all multiples of k in the set 2 to n.

   - Solution 3 (Sieve of Eratosthenes): Allocate a process to delete all multiples of 2. Whenever a number is discovered to be prime by all existing processes, allocate a new process to delete all multiples of this prime.

   - Solution 4: Divide the set into i blocks of size n/i. Allocate a process to each block. Begin computing the primes in the first block. When a prime k has been computed, we can release all processes containing numbers up to k^2.

1.7   Further Reading

Concurrent programming was originally developed within the context of multiprogramming operating systems and most books on the subject contain chapters on concurrent programming ([Dei85], [PS85]). Interest in parallel algorithms is increasing since the introduction of parallel computers. [Qui87] describes algorithms for these computers.

1.8   Exercises

1. Given partial results of the sort procedures $(0, 3)$ and $(1, 2)$, can the merge procedure immediately create the partial result $(0, 1, 2, 3)$?

2. Describe a concurrent version of Quicksort.

Chapter 2

The Concurrent Programming Abstraction

2.1 Introduction

Scientific ·descriptions of the world are based on abstractions. One creates an idealized model of some phenomenon and then proceeds to study a higher-level complex system. For example, a human body is described in medical science as a system constructed of organs, bones, nerves, etc. All of these are made up of *cells*, but a physician does not usually need to reason about the properties of individual cells in order to make a diagnosis. Continuing down the scale of abstractions, cells are composed of *molecules* which are composed of *atoms* which are composed of *elementary particles*. As the level of abstraction descends, the abstractions studied become more mathematical since the 'actual' atoms and elementary particles can only be directly perceived under expensive laboratory conditions. It is beyond human ability to make a medical diagnosis based on the quantum theory of atoms, even though the illness is ultimately caused by interactions among the atoms.

In computer science, abstractions are just as important. A programming language is nothing more than an abstraction which is designed to ignore the details of specific machine instructions and architectures. Descending in level of abstraction, we find:

Operating systems An operating system defines a set of systems services, like a file system and operations to access it. The operating system can be implemented on different computers.

Instruction sets Most computer manufacturers design and build families of CPUs which execute the same instruction set as seen by the assembler programmer or compiler writer. The members of a family may be implemented in totally different ways – emulating some instructions in software or using memory for registers.

Integrated circuits Thousands or hundreds of thousands of circuit elements can be packed in one small 'chip'. The abstraction is the description of the behavior of the chip as seen from a few dozen connector pins. Competitors may build a totally different circuit implementing the same abstraction.

Electromagnetics The behavior of individual circuit elements is described by mathematical models such as Ohm's law and Maxwell's equations dealing with currents, voltages and fields.

Electronics This behavior is explained by the properties of electrons flowing in conductors, semiconductors and insulators.

Quantum theory This theory explains why the electron flow should behave as it does in materials made of different atomic elements.

Again, what is important to understand is that we could never describe the effect of `X:=X+1` directly in terms of the behavior of the electrons within the 'chip' implementing the computer which is executing the statement.

Abstractions are of overwhelming importance in software, though this was not obvious in the early days of programming. Software systems are the most complex systems ever built in terms of the number of different components and the complexity of their interconnection. Two of the most important techniques used in creating software abstractions are encapsulation and concurrency.

Encapsulation acheives abstraction by dividing a software module into a public specification and a hidden implementation. The specification describes the available operations on a data structure or real-world model. The detailed software implementation of the structure or model is written within a separate section that is not accessible outside the module. Thus changes in the internal data representation and algorithm can be made without affecting the programming of the rest of the system. Modern programming languages like Ada directly support encapsulation.

Concurrent programming is an abstraction that is designed to make it possible to reason about the dynamic behavior of programs. This abstraction will be carefully explained in the rest of this chapter.

An objection may be made against abstractions in general, and against concurrent programming in particular, namely that real-world objects are not so neat. If so, the abstraction may be irrelevant for engineering a real system. There are two parts to the answer. The first part is that abstractions are carefully chosen so as to be as close as possible to reality. Otherwise, the abstraction is wrong and a different one must be invented. Secondly, abstractions form the scientific basis upon which the engineer works. In fact the work of an engineer might be described as choosing the best abstraction and implementing it in a way that solves the problem. 'Best' may involve criteria such as cost, performance, reliability, deadlines, etc. It is much easier to modify a known concept to meet some criterion than it is to develop a new concept for each problem. Abstractions are as important to a software engineer as differential equations are to a hardware engineer even though there are no 'ideal' components in either field.

2.2 Interleaving

Concurrent programming abstraction is the study of interleaved execution sequences of the atomic instructions of sequential processes.

As discussed in the first chapter, a concurrent program consists of a set of sequential processes executing simultaneously. Each process is an 'ordinary' program with its own code and data and is considered to be executed on a computer which consists of a CPU, memory, and I/O channels. A *distributed* system is a computer system with more than one computer. The computers are connected together and can exchange messages or access each other's memory. If we have one computer for each process, then the correspondence between the abstraction and reality is very close.

However, even if the concurrent program is being executed by sharing the resources of one computer, it is still convenient to consider each process as executing simultaneously. The alternative would be to consider the program as one process which happens to be composed of several modules. The problem with this alternative is the combinatorial explosion of possible program states. For example, in our concurrent Mergesort program (Figure 1.7), let us suppose that each of the three procedures contains ten instructions. We would have to consider $10^3 = 1000$ different possible states of the program. In the case of an operating system, it would not even be possible to predict what computation will be done by each process since the processes ('jobs') are written by programmers working independently.

Thus in our abstraction, each process is considered to be operating on its own processor, executing its own program. We will only have to consider possible interaction in two cases:

Contention Two processes compete for the same resource: computing resources in general, or access to a particular memory cell or channel in particular.

Communication Two processes may need to communicate causing information to be passed from one to the other. Even the mere fact of communication can be important because it allows the processes to *synchronize*: to agree that a certain event has taken place.

So far, we have a set of processes executing simultaneously on a set of processors. These processors can be operating at arbitrary speeds and responding to arbitrary external signals. A further abstraction is to ignore time and to consider only the sequences of instructions as executed by each process. The sequence of instructions depicted in the upper line in Figure 2.1 have different execution times and these vary from one computer to another. We will model them by the sequence in the lower line of the figure where each instruction takes a fixed amount of time. In fact, since the time interval is fixed, we ignore the time scale

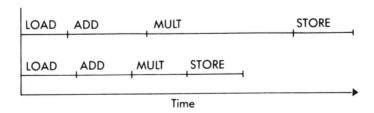

Figure 2.1 Execution sequences

(say, microseconds) and consider the execution of one instruction to be one unit of 'time'.

The justification for this abstraction is that as far as the *correctness* of a program is concerned, the absolute time of execution is not relevant. If we have instructions End_Print and Start_Print in processes $P1$ and $P2$, respectively, it is important that End_Print be executed before and not during or after the execution of Start_Print but it should not make a difference if End_Print were executed 10 milliseconds or 10 seconds before Start_Print.

This abstraction is the hardest one to accept, especially if one has experience with time-critical systems like real-time controllers or operating systems. In these systems, the specification of the program typically contains absolute time requirements: 'update the position of the aircraft on the radar screen within 0.5 seconds'. There are several justifications for the use of execution sequences as the basic model rather than absolute time:

- Execution sequences are appropriate for reasoning about properties other than absolute timing requirements. For most requirements, absolute time would introduce a complexity which is not necessary.

- Systems are always being upgraded with faster components and even faster algorithms. If the correctness of a concurrent program depended on absolute time, every modification to the hardware or software would require that the system be rechecked for correctness. For example, suppose that an operating system was correct under the assumption that characters are being typed in at no more that 10 characters per terminal per second. That is a conservative assumption for a human typist that would be invalidated if a new terminal was installed that did local editing and sent the data on the screen to the computer at 100 characters per second.

- Most time functions, like interrupts from a hardware timer, are actually events that fit into the execution sequence model. Thus, aside from requirements on response time, it is usually possible to deal with time in the model.

In the end, however, the concurrent programming model of execution sequences must be carefully applied or possibly modified or extended when used in systems with absolute time requirements.

The abstraction that ignores absolute speed in a single process is extended so that all the execution sequences of all the processes are *interleaved* into a single execution sequence. Given two instructions $I1$ and $I2$ in two processes $P1$ and $P2$, we can distinguish two cases (Figure 2.2):

1. $end(I1) \leq begin(I2)$
2. $begin(I2) < end(I1)$

The first case is obviously compatible with the concept of a single execution sequence. We forbid the second case by restricting our model so that the effect of two simultaneous instructions is required to be the same as *either* of the two possible sequences obtained by executing the instructions one after the other.

Digital equipment is designed so that any bit of memory or any signal is considered to have one of two binary values. In case of contention, like two

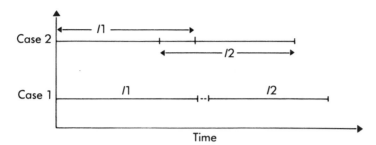

Figure 2.2 Simultaneous execution of instructions

attempts to write to the same memory cell, or two peripherals trying to cause an interrupt, the hardware resolves the situation in a manner compatible with our restriction.

Even in the case of a distributed system, it may be true that two instructions are executed simultaneously on two different computers, but we can arbitrarily assign them an order with no effect on the computation unless there is contention or communication. If the two instructions attempt to access the same hardware, this must be resolved by the hardware. If they send messages on a communications line, we assume an underlying protocol that correctly delivers the messages, though possibly in some arbitrary order.

The model is not as restricted as it might seem on first glance. *Arbitrary* interleavings are allowed. One process could complete hundreds of instructions before any other process executes one instruction. Or we could have a perfect interleaving of one instruction at a time from each process.

A concurrent program is required to be correct under *all* interleavings.

Then, if the computer hardware is changed or if the rate of incoming signals changes, we may have a different interleaving, but the program is still correct.

Furthermore, any concurrent program that depends on external signals is difficult, if not impossible, to repeat exactly. A concurrent program cannot be 'debugged' in the familiar sense of diagnosing a problem, correcting it and re-running the program to check if the bug still exists. We may just execute a different interleaving in which the bug does not exist. The solution is to develop programming and verification techniques that ensure that a program is correct under all interleavings.

The only constraint to arbitrary interleaving is that *fairness* must be preserved. At every point in the interleaved sequence, *eventually* instructions from each process must be included. It should be intuitively clear that all this is saying is that no processor in a distributed system is infinitely slow, or that no process in a shared system is deferred forever.

A convenient device for reasoning about concurrent programs is to assume that given the instruction sequences of a set of processes, a *scheduler* is in charge of constructing the interleaving. If we are trying to show that a program is incorrect, we take the part of the scheduler and construct a 'bad' interleaving whose behavior does not meet the problem specification. To prove that a program is correct is more difficult – we must show that no matter how malicious the scheduler is, the behavior of the program is correct.

2.3   Atomic Instructions

The concurrent programming abstraction deals with interleaved sequences of atomic instructions. In applying the abstraction, it is extremely important to define exactly what instructions are being interleaved. For example, suppose that a memory cell represented by an integer variable is being incremented by two processes (Figure 2.3). If the compiler translates the high-level language statement into a single INC instruction, *any* interleaving of the instruction sequences of the two processes will give the same value (Figure 2.4). On the other hand, if all computation is done in registers,[1] the compiled code would look like Figure 2.5. The same figure shows that some interleavings give the wrong answer.

```
N: Integer := 0;

task body P1 is
begin
  N := N + 1;
end P1;

task body P2 is
begin
  N := N + 1;
end P2;
```

Figure 2.3 Two processes incrementing a variable

Process	Instruction	Value of N
(Initially)		0
P1	INC N	1
P2	INC N	2

Process	Instruction	Value of N
(Initially)		0
P2	INC N	1
P1	INC N	2

Figure 2.4 Computer with INC instruction

Thus the correctness of a concurrent program depends on the atomic instructions used by the computer or system on which it runs. In this book, the emphasis

---

[1] Each process is assumed to have a separate set of registers.

Process	Instruction	N	Reg(1)	Reg(2)
(Initially)		0	-	-
P1	LOAD Reg, N	0	0	-
P2	LOAD Reg, N	0	0	0
P1	ADD Reg, #1	0	1	0
P2	ADD Reg, #1	0	1	1
P1	STORE Reg, N	1	1	1
P2	STORE Reg, N	1	1	1

Figure 2.5 Computer with registers

is not so much on solving a variety of problems as on solving a few typical problems under a wide variety of assumptions about the underlying atomic instructions. The range of possibilities reflects a basic conflict in the design of computer hardware and software. If the instructions are simple, the implementation will be simple and presumably efficient and inexpensive. However, the instructions will be hard to use. If the atomic instructions are more powerful and expressive, it will be easier to write correct programs, but the implementation will be more difficult.

The example of Figure 2.3 illustrates that it is harder to write a correct program for a computer that must do arithmetic in a register than for one which can compute directly to memory.

The atomic instructions used in Part I assume the existence of common memory accessible to all processes. Common memory can be used in two ways which differ only in what is accessed by the processes:

- Global data which may be read and written by more than one process.
- Object code of operating system routines which may be called more than one process.

In Part II we assume only that each process can send a message to another process.

Common memory instructions are easy and efficient to implement on a single computer being shared by the various processes. Message passing is needed in distributed systems. In many cases, we will show how one atomic instruction can be emulated by an algorithm written using another instruction. The emulations may not be efficient or simple but they give a feeling for the tradeoffs between expressiveness and simplicity.

The first atomic instruction studied is Load-Store to common memory. This is the model shown in Figure 2.5 where *every* access to a global variable is a single instruction and interleaving is permitted between any two accesses. On the other hand, an attempt to simultaneously access a variable is resolved as an interleaving, not as a garbage value. It is possible to weaken this assumption even further (and on one occasion we shall do so), but in most practical applications this is as low-level as necessary.

Load-Store is not very powerful and solutions to concurrent programming problems that use this primitive are not efficient. Most concurrent programs are written on machines that support complex instructions (like INC) or high-level primitives implemented on an underlying operating system.

2.4   Correctness

For sequential programs, the concept of *correctness* is so familiar that the formal definition is often neglected. For concurrent programs, it is imperative to formalize correctness, both because the concepts are very different and often unintuitive, and because formal verification of correctness is often crucial.

There are two definitions of correctness for programs that are supposed to terminate. Let $P(\vec{x})$ be a property of the input variables $\vec{x}$ and $Q(\vec{x}, \vec{y})$ be a property of the input variables $\vec{x}$ and output variables $\vec{y}$. Then for any values $\vec{a}$ of the input variables, we define correctness as follows:

Partial correctness If $P(\vec{a})$ is true *and* the program terminates when started with $\vec{a}$ as the values of the input variables $\vec{x}$, then $Q(\vec{a}, \vec{b})$ is true where $\vec{b}$ are the values of the output variables upon termination.

$$(P(\vec{a}) \wedge terminates(Prog(\vec{a}, \vec{b}))) \supset Q(\vec{a}, \vec{b}) \qquad (2.1)$$

Total correctness As in partial correctness, but we require the program to terminate.

$$P(\vec{a}) \supset (terminates(Prog(\vec{a}, \vec{b})) \wedge Q(\vec{a}, \vec{b})) \qquad (2.2)$$

To give a trivial example, if `SQR(x,y)` is a program that computes the square root of `x` and stores it into the variable `y`, the two specifications of correctness give:

$$(a \geq 0 \wedge terminates(SQR(a, b))) \supset b = \sqrt{a} \qquad (2.3)$$

$$a \geq 0 \supset (terminates(SQR(a, b)) \wedge b = \sqrt{a}) \qquad (2.4)$$

Note that the behavior of the program on negative numbers is irrelevant. If we were concerned about the behavior of the program when negative numbers are input, the specification of correctness would have to be changed accordingly. Note also that a program that always goes into an infinite loop is partially correct for this specification (in fact, it is partially correct for *all* specifications).

Partial correctness and total correctness are appropriate for concurrent programs which terminate just as for sequential programs. But when specifying non-terminating programs such as operating systems or real-time controllers, we need other definitions. If one of these systems terminates, we consider it a bug!

Correctness of concurrent programs is defined in terms of properties of execution sequences. Such a property is (implicitly) prefixed by: 'for all possible execution sequences'. This was discussed earlier in the chapter as a means of modeling different relative speeds of the processors as well as the non-repeatability of concurrent programs.

There are two types of correctness properties:

Safety properties The property must *always* be true.

Liveness properties The property must *eventually* be true ('now' is included in 'eventually').

The most common safety property is *mutual exclusion*: two processes may not interleave certain (sub-)sequences of instructions. Instead, one sequence must be completed before the other commences. The order in which the sequences are executed is *not* important. This models many problems in operating systems such as access to resources like printers and access to system-wide data and services. It must *always* be true that at most one process access a printer at any one instant. It is inconceivable that an operating system could be considered correct if it ever assigned a printer to two processes, even if only momentarily and even if only under unlikely circumstances.

The other important safety property is absence of *deadlock*. A non-terminating system must always be able to proceed doing useful work. A system which cannot respond to any signal or request is deadlocked and again, this must never happen. A system may be quiescent if there is nothing to do, but in that case, it is usually actively executing a background idle-process or self-test and it will be able to respond instantly to an interrupt. A deadlocked system will not respond, or as the slang goes, the system is 'hung'.

Like partial correctness which can be satisfied by any non-terminating program, a program which does nothing will satisfy most safety properties. A program which never assigns a printer to any process will trivially not assign one to two processes. In order for something to actually happen, liveness properties must be specified. For example, if a process posts a request to print, *eventually* it will be assigned a printer. The technical term is *absence of (individual) starvation*. This is a weak specification because a program that assigned a printer after a thousand years would still be correct, but we have already justified ignoring absolute time. If the system is not malicious, 'eventually' will be relatively soon unless there is contention for the printer.

A particular type of liveness property is called a *fairness property*. If there is contention, we will often want to specify how the contention must be resolved. Four possible specifications of fairness are:

Weak fairness If a process continuously makes a request, eventually it will be granted.

Strong fairness If a process makes a request infinitely often, eventually it will be granted.

Linear waiting If a process makes a request, it will be granted before any other process is granted the request more than once.

FIFO (first-in first-out) If a process makes a request, it will be granted before that of any process making a later request.

The difference between strong and weak fairness is shown in Figure 2.6. A process requests a service by setting a flag to 1. The upper line shows process P1 periodically issuing a request and then canceling the request whereas process P2 depicted in the lower line issues a request and holds it outstanding for an indefinite period. The process granting the requests checks the flag periodically at times $t0, t1, t2, \ldots$. As shown, this system is weakly-fair because it will grant P2's request but not strongly-fair since it will not grant P1's request. Even though P1 makes its request infinitely often, the server may check the outstanding requests exactly when P1 is not requesting. A strongly-fair system *would* grant P1's request.

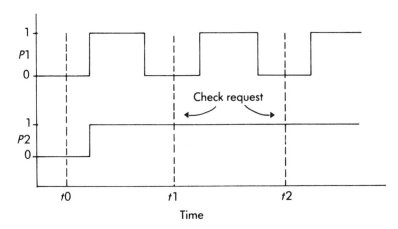

Figure 2.6 Strong and weak fairness

These two concepts of fairness are not very practical because they depend on 'eventually' and 'infinitely often'. Linear waiting is a practical concept because it says that once a process has issued a request, it may be overtaken by every other process, but only once. If we know what the longest permitted print job is, we can calculate a bound on the length of time a process must wait to be assigned a printer.

FIFO is the strongest specification of fairness. It is simple to implement on centralized systems. On a distributed system, it is not clear what 'later' means, so weaker definitions of fairness are important.

2.5   Inductive Proofs of Correctness

A safety property of a concurrent program holds if it is true at every state of every execution sequence. A non-terminating program is potentially infinite and there are an infinite number of execution sequences since at each step the scheduler could choose an instruction from any process to create the interleaving. How can one prove properties of infinite objects?

The answer is proof by induction. Let us recall how this works in mathematics before describing the technique for programs. If a property $P(n)$ is to hold for all natural numbers n (i.e. for all $n \geq 0$), we prove it in two steps:

Basis Prove $P(0)$.

Inductive step Assume that $P(n)$ is true (the *inductive hypothesis*) and prove $P(n+1)$.

Intuitively, if $P(0)$ is true, by the inductive step applied once, $P(1)$ is true. Now assuming this as the inductive hypothesis, we prove $P(2)$. There is no bound on the value of n for which we can prove $P(n)$, so $P(n)$ is true for all n.

The inductive proof technique is valid for any sequence of values that can be put into one-to-one correspondence with the natural numbers: $i_0, i_1, \ldots$. In particular, we can use it to prove that a property holds *always* during an execution sequence:

Basis Prove the property for the initial state of the program.

Inductive step Assume that the property holds after the nth step of the execution sequence (the inductive hypothesis) and prove that it holds after the $(n+1)^{\text{st}}$ step.

But we do not know what the execution sequence is until the scheduler actually chooses a process whose instruction will be executed next. So we are required to prove that if the inductive hypothesis holds in any state, it will continue to hold in *each* state that can be reached by executing a statement of any process. Since any execution sequence can be constructed as an interleaving of the individual execution sequences, the property holds since the induction holds for each choice made by the scheduler. A property which is true for each state of every possible execution sequence is called an *invariant*.

Figure 2.7 is a trivial program designed to demonstrate the technique. We want to prove that $P \equiv X = 0 \lor X = 1$ is an invariant. It is impossible to prove this directly. Obviously, it is true initially. Assuming that P is true in any state, we have to prove that P remains true after any instruction of the program is executed. Suppose we are at a state where process $P1$ is about to execute X := X+1. Using our knowledge of the semantics of the assignment statement, we can conclude that $X = 1 \lor X = 2$, which is not what we want.

As usual with inductive proofs, the solution is to prove a stronger claim than the required property. The invariant will include formulas $at(l)$ expressing the value of the instruction pointer of a process. $at(l)$ means that the location l is the next instruction to be executed by that process.

Theorem 2.5.1 $Q \equiv (at(a1) \supset X = 0) \land (at(b1) \supset X = 1)$ *is an invariant.*

Proof: Initially, process $P1$ is $at(a1)$ and the value of X is 0, so Q is true.

Assume that Q is true in any state. There are four possible transitions in the program. For each one we will prove that Q remains true following the transition.

1. $a1 \rightarrow b1$: By the inductive hypothesis, when $P1$ is $at(a1)$, then $X = 0$. Following the transition, $at(b1)$ is true, but so is $X = 1$ by the semantics of the assignment statement.

2. $b1 \to a1$: By the inductive hypothesis, $X = 1$. Following the transition, $at(a1)$ and $X = 0$ are true.

3. $a2 \to b2$: A transition in $P2$ does not affect the location counter of $P1$ nor the value of X. Since the truth of Q depends only on these values, the inductive hypothesis trivially implies that Q is still true.

4. $b2 \to a2$: As in (3). □

```
task body P1 is
   X: Integer := 0;
begin
   loop
a1:   X := X + 1;
b1:   X := X - 1;
   end loop;
end P1;

task body P2 is
   Y: Integer := 0;
begin
   loop
a2:   Y := Y + 1;
b2:   Y := Y - 1;
   end loop;
end P2;
```

Figure 2.7 Inductive proofs of correctness

Since $at(a1) \lor at(b1)$ is true, theorem 2.5.1 implies that P is invariant.

Note that (1) and (2) require reasoning only on process $P1$, and (3) and (4) only on $P2$. This shows how concurrent programming solves combinatorial explosion since we need to prove the invariant on a number of cases equal to the sum and not the product of the number of instructions in each process. (3) and (4) are called proof of *non-interference* since they show that $P2$ cannot interfere with $P1$.

In many cases, proofs can be simplified using elementary propositional logic. An implication $P \supset Q$ is true if and only if the *antecedent* P is false or the *consequent* Q is true. It will remain true, unless P and Q are both false and P 'suddenly' becomes true by executing a statement, or P and Q are both true and Q 'suddenly' becomes false. Many inductive formulas will take the form of an implication:

$$at(location) \supset variable = value$$

If it is assumed true then it could only become false on a transition to *location* when *variable* $\neq$ *value* or a transition by another process that causes the consequent to become false while this process is in *location*.

2.6 Liveness proofs

To prove liveness properties is more complicated in that the formalism is more complicated. On the other hand, one need only prove that a certain state must eventually occur on any execution sequence. The arguments are based on the assumed fairness of the underlying scheduler and the eventuality properties of the various program constructs.

For example, we prove that if process $P1$ in Figure 2.7 is $at(a1)$ then eventually it will be at $at(b1)$. Eventually, process $P1$ must be scheduled and we assume that an assignment statement always terminates. Thus eventually $P1$ will be $at(b1)$.

In discussing liveness we will use the following notation:

- $\Box p$ means p is *always* true.
- $\Diamond p$ means p is *eventually* true.

These are operators of a formal logic called *temporal logic* which facilitates reasoning on propositions that change with time. In particular, it can be used to reason about programs which change with time. Thus $\Box p$ means that at every subsequent point in the execution sequence, p is true. This is what we have called an invariant. $\Diamond p$ means that at some future moment in the execution sequence, p is true (where future includes 'now'). The formula from the previous paragraph can be written: $at(a1) \supset \Diamond at(b1)$. A useful formula is $\Diamond \Box p$ which means that at some future moment, p will be true and will stay that way forever.

A formal development of temporal logic is beyond the scope of this book. In the following proofs in temporal logic, use common-sense reasoning as if these operators were just convenient abbreviations for natural language. For example, from $\Diamond \Box p$ and $\Diamond \Box q$, we can deduce $\Diamond \Box (p \wedge q)$. As shown in Figure 2.8, eventually one formula, say p, must be held true and then eventually q must be held true while p is (obviously) still held true. Thus from that moment on, both p and q will be true.

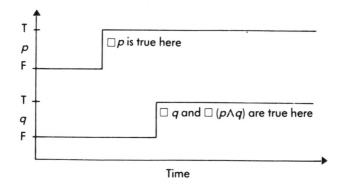

Figure 2.8 Example in temporal logic

Liveness proofs are difficult when there are conditional statements: `if B then S1 else S2`. We can assume that eventually we will execute either statement S1 or statement S2 but we cannot know which without more information on the boolean expression B. Even if B is eventually true ($\Diamond B$), it might be true only momentarily and the scheduler may execute the conditional statement before or after this state. To conclude that eventually S1 is executed ($\Diamond at(S1)$), we must first prove an invariant showing that the value of B will be held true indefinitely or that eventually such an invariant becomes true ($\Diamond \Box B$).

2.7   Further Reading

The interleaving model is standard in the literature on concurrent programming. For a different view based on relativity see [Lam86]. [Gri81] is a comprehensive text on verification of sequential programs. Inductive proofs of concurrent programs are from [OG76], and the temporal logic of concurrent programs is from [MP81]. [Fra86] is a research monograph on the difficult subject of fairness.

2.8   Exercises

1. Enumerate all the possible interleavings of instructions in the program in Figure 2.3 under the register model of computation. Note which interleavings give the correct answer.

2. Estimate the number of possible interleavings of concurrent Mergesort as a function of the size of the array.

3. Estimate the number of possible interleavings of concurrent matrix multiplication assuming that each element of the result matrix is computed by a separate process.

4. Draw a diagram similar to Figure 2.8 for: $\Box\Diamond\Box p$ and $\Diamond\Box\Diamond p$. What relations exist between those formulas and $\Box\Diamond p$ and $\Diamond\Box p$?

5. Which of the following are true? In each case draw a diagram justifying your answer.

    (a) $\Box(p \land q) \supset (\Box p \land \Box q)$

    (b) $(\Box p \land \Box q) \supset \Box(p \land q)$

    (c) $\Diamond(p \land q) \supset (\Diamond p \land \Diamond q)$

    (d) $(\Diamond p \land \Diamond q) \supset \Diamond(p \land q)$

    (e) $\Box(p \lor q) \supset (\Box p \lor \Box q)$

    (f) $(\Box p \lor \Box q) \supset \Box(p \lor q)$

    (g) $\Diamond(p \lor q) \supset (\Diamond p \lor \Diamond q)$

    (h) $(\Diamond p \lor \Diamond q) \supset \Diamond(p \lor q)$

Chapter 3

The Mutual Exclusion Problem

3.1 Introduction

This chapter presents solutions to the mutual exclusion problem. First we will solve the problem for two processes using Load-Store to common memory as the only atomic instructions. Solutions will then be given for N processes using Load-Store and then using more complex atomic instructions.

One solution to the mutual exclusion problem for two processes is called Dekker's algorithm. This algorithm will be developed in a step-by-step sequence of incorrect algorithms. Each of these incorrect algorithms will demonstrate some pathological behavior that is typical of concurrent algorithms. Formal proofs of properties of the algorithms will be emphasized.

The mutual exclusion problem for N processes:

1. N processes are executing in a infinite loop a sequence of instructions which can be divided into to subsequences: the critical section and the non-critical section. The program must satisfy the *mutual exclusion property*: instructions from the critical sections of two or more processes must not be interleaved.

2. The solution will be described by inserting into the loop additional instructions that are to be executed by a process wishing to enter and leave its critical section – the *pre-protocol* and *post-protocol*, respectively (Figure 3.1). These protocols may require additional variables.

```
loop
  Non_Critical_Section;
  Pre_Protocol;
  Critical_Section;
  Post_Protocol;
end loop;
```

Figure 3.1 Form of mutual exclusion solution

3. A process may halt in its non-critical section. It may not halt during execution of its protocols or critical section. If one process halts in its non-critical section,

it must not interfere with other processes.

4. The program must not deadlock. If *some* processes are trying to enter their critical section then *one* of them must eventually succeed. There may be local progress within the protocols as the processes set and check the protocol variables, but if no process ever succeeds in making the transition from pre-protocol to critical section, we say that the program is deadlocked.

5. There must be no starvation of one of the processes. If a process indicates its intention to enter the critical section by commencing the execution of the pre-protocol, *eventually* it will succeed. This is a very strong requirement in that it must be shown that *no* possible execution sequence of the program, no matter how improbable, can cause starvation.

6. In the absence of contention for the critical section, a single process wishing to enter its critical section will succeed. Not only will it succeed, but a good solution to the mutual exclusion problem will have minimal overhead in this case.

The solution may assume that load and store to common memory are atomic. This will be indicated by declaring variables that are global to both processes and allowing either process to store the variable by assignment `C1:=1`, or to load the value of the variable. Syntactically, a load will be indicated by having the variable appear in an expression in the right-hand side of an assignment statement `C2:=C1` or in an expression used in a conditional statement `if C1=1 then`. In the event of a simultaneous load and store, the effect is to interleave the two instructions in an arbitrary order.

3.2 First Attempt

In a first attempt at solving the mutual exclusion problem for two processes (Figure 3.2), we define a single global variable `Turn` which can take the two values 1 and 2. Initially, `Turn` has an arbitrary value, say 1. The variable indicates whose 'turn' it is to enter the critical section. A process wishing to enter the critical section will execute a pre-protocol consisting of a statement that loops until the value of `Turn` indicates that its turn has arrived. Upon exiting the critical section, the process sets the value of `Turn` to the number of the other process.

Notation: `Turn` refers to the variable in the algorithm. $Turn$ is used to denote the value of that variable in a formula like $Turn = 1$. A similar distinction is made for other variables.

Theorem 3.2.1 *This solution satisfies the mutual exclusion requirement.*

Proof: A formal inductive proof is left as an exercise that may be done after studying the technique in the proof of the third attempt. Here we give an informal proof.

Suppose, to the contrary, that at some point in the execution sequence both processes are in their critical sections. Without loss of generality, P1 entered its

```
Turn: Integer range 1..2 := 1;

task body P1 is
begin
  loop
    Non_Critical_Section_1;
    loop exit when Turn = 1; end loop;
    Critical_Section_1;
    Turn := 2;
  end loop;
end P1;

task body P2 is
begin
  loop
    Non_Critical_Section_2;
    loop exit when Turn = 2; end loop;
    Critical_Section_2;
    Turn := 1;
  end loop;
end P2;
```

Figure 3.2 First attempt

critical section before P2. That is, P1 entered its critical section at time $t1$, P2 entered its critical section at time $t2$, $t1 < t2$, and during this time interval, P1 remained in its critical section. Now at time $t1$, $Turn = 1$ so that P1 was able to exit its loop statement. Similarly, at time $t2$, $Turn = 2$. But during the interval from $t1$ to $t2$, P1 remained in its critical section and did not execute the post-protocol, which is the only statement that can assign the value 2 to Turn. Thus the value of Turn at $t2$ must still be 1, contradicting our previous statement. □

Let us examine this proof to see where the assumptions of the concurrent programming model have been used. The assumption that instructions are interleaved means that the processes cannot enter their critical sections simultaneously. If they try to enter simultaneously, they will be interleaved in some arbitrary order. We must prove that the requirement is satisfied under either order. However, given the symmetry of the solution (both processes execute identical programs except for the process number), it is sufficient to prove the theorem for one of the two possibilities.

The assumption that load and store are atomic instructions allows us to claim that the value of Turn must be either 1 or 2 and that it can only change when explicitly assigned.

Theorem 3.2.2 *The solution cannot deadlock.*

Proof: For the program to deadlock, both processes must execute the test on Turn in the loop infinitely often and fail. Then from P1, we can deduce that

$Turn = 2$ and from P2, $Turn = 1$, which is impossible. $\square$

Theorem 3.2.3 *There is no starvation.*

Proof: For starvation to exist, one process, say P1, must enter its critical section infinitely often, while the other process executes its pre-protocol forever without succeeding in entering its critical section. But if P1 executes its critical section even once, it will set Turn to 2 in its post-protocol. Then the next time that P2 is allowed to execute, it will succeed in entering its critical section. $\square$

Theorem 3.2.4 *The solution can fail in the absence of contention.*

Proof: Suppose that P2 halts in the non-critical section. Then the value of Turn will never again be changed from 2 to 1. So process P1 may enter its critical section at most one more time. Once P1 has set Turn to 2, it will never again be able to succeed in the test in its pre-protocol. $\square$

Theorem 3.2.4 shows that we have not solved the mutual exclusion problem because one of the required properties does not hold. In fact, even if both processes can be guaranteed not to halt, we must reject this solution. If P1 needs to enter its critical section several times per second, while P2 is content to enter once per hour, this solution would not solve the problem. The processes are coerced into working at the same rate.

The explicit passing of the right to execute is a well-known programming technique called *coroutines*. This technique is useful when a single problem is to be solved by several modules working together. We are interested in systems that involve several loosely-coupled processes working on independent problems simultaneously or different aspects of a single problem. We explicitly wish to refrain from making assumptions on the relative speed of the various processes. For this, coroutines are not sufficient and the full power of concurrent programming techniques is needed.

3.3   Second Attempt

The previous solution is incorrect because both processes are setting and testing a single global variable. Thus if one process dies, the other is blocked. Let us try to remedy this situation by providing each process with its own variable (Figure 3.3). The interpretation that should be placed on the variable is: $Ci = 0$ if Pi wishes to enter its critical section. Ci will be set by Pi before it enters its critical section and reset upon completion of its critical section. It will be tested by the other process which will loop until the critical section may be safely entered. If a process is halted in its non-critical section, the value of its variable will remain at 1 and the other process will always succeed in immediately entering its critical section.

Unfortunately, the program does not even satisfy the mutual exclusion requirement.

```
                    C1, C2: Integer range 0..1 := 1;

              task body P1 is
              begin
                loop
                  Non_Critical_Section_1;
                  loop exit when C2 = 1; end loop;
                  C1 := 0;
                  Critical_Section_1;
                  C1 := 1;
                end loop;
              end P1;

              task body P2 is
              begin
                loop
                  Non_Critical_Section_2;
                  loop exit when C1 = 1; end loop;
                  C2 := 0;
                  Critical_Section_2;
                  C2 := 1;
                end loop;
              end P2;
```

Figure 3.3 Second attempt

Theorem 3.3.1 P1 *and* P2 *can be in their critical sections simultaneously.*

Proof: Consider the following interleaving of instructions of the two processes beginning with the initial state

1. P1 checks C2 and finds $C2 = 1$.
2. P2 checks C1 and finds $C1 = 1$.
3. P1 sets C1 to 0.
4. P2 sets C2 to 0.
5. P1 enters its critical section.
6. P2 enters its critical section.

This violates the mutual exclusion requirement. □

It is extremely important to note the difference between this proof and the proof that the first attempt does satisfy mutual exclusion. Since this property is a safety property, it must be satisfied for *all* possible execution sequences. Thus we need a mathematical argument to prove it because the number of execution sequences is infinite. To show that the property is false, however, it is sufficient to describe one execution sequence for which it fails.

3.4   Third Attempt

In the second attempt, we introduced the variables Ci which are intended to indicate when process Pi is in its critical section. However, once a process has successfully completed its loop statement, it cannot be prevented from entering its critical section. Thus the state of a computation reached after the loop and before the assignment to Ci is effectively part of the critical section, yet Ci still does not indicate this fact. The third attempt (Figure 3.4) recognizes that the loop should be considered part of the critical section by moving the assignment to Ci before the loop.

```
         C1, C2: Integer range 0..1 := 1;

         task body P1 is
         begin
           loop
         a1:   Non_Critical_Section_1;
         b1:   C1 := 0;
         c1:   loop exit when C2 = 1; end loop;
         d1:   Critical_Section_1;
         e1:   C1 := 1;
           end loop;
         end P1;

         task body P2 is
         begin
           loop
         a2:   Non_Critical_Section_2;
         b2:   C2 := 0;
         c2:   loop exit when C1 = 1; end loop;
         d2:   Critical_Section_2;
         e2:   C2 := 1;
           end loop;
         end P2;
```

Figure 3.4 Third attempt

Theorem 3.4.1 *The solution satisfies the mutual exclusion property.*

Proof: The proof will be by induction on the execution sequence. We claim that the following formulas are invariant.

$$C1 = 0 \equiv at(c1) \vee at(d1) \vee at(e1) \tag{3.1}$$
$$C2 = 0 \equiv at(c2) \vee at(d2) \vee at(e2) \tag{3.2}$$
$$\neg(at(d1) \wedge at(d2)) \tag{3.3}$$

Proof of 3.1: Formula 3.1 is initially true because the initial value of C1 is 1 and initially, $at(a1)$ is true, hence both sides of the equivalence are false.

Assume by induction that the formula is true and consider every possible transition that the program can make.

1. $a1 \rightarrow b1$: This transition does not affect the truth of any formula in the invariant. Hence, if it was true before executing this instruction, it is still true.

2. $b1 \rightarrow c1$: This makes the left-hand side of the equivalence true by assigning 0 to C1. It also makes the disjunction on the right-hand side true, because now $at(c1)$ is true.

3. $c1 \rightarrow c1$: This transition means that we execute the test in the loop and fail to exit. This does not affect the truth of left-hand side because C1 is not assigned. The right-hand side remains true.

4. $d1 \rightarrow e1$: As in the previous transition.

5. $e1 \rightarrow a1$: This makes the left-hand side false by assignment and the right-hand side false by the transition out of e1.

6. Any transition in P2. Obviously, C1 is not assigned and the location counter of P1 is not affected by a transition in P2.

Thus we have shown that formula 3.1 is initially true and that following *any* transition of the program (in either process) it remains true. Hence, the formula is an invariant of the computation.

The above proof is done in full detail so that the concept of inductive proofs can be understood. In practice, a more concise argument would suffice:

Proof of 3.1: The formula is true initially. The only transitions that could affect the truth of the formula are the transitions: $b1 \rightarrow c1$ and $e1 \rightarrow a1$. Now show that the two assignments to C1 also cause the location counter to change to preserve the truth of the formula. □

The invariance of 3.2 follows by a symmetric proof. It remains to prove the invariance of 3.3.

Proof of 3.3: The formula is trivially true initially because the initial locations are $a1$ and $a2$. The only transitions that could possibly falsify the formula are $c2 \rightarrow d2$ while $at(d1)$ is true or symmetrically the transition in P2. In words, P1 is in its critical section and then P2 enters.

By invariant 3.1, $at(d1) \supset C1 = 0$. Then it is impossible for the transition $c2 \rightarrow d2$ to occur because the condition in the loop requires $C1 = 1$. By a symmetric argument, we can prove that the transition in P2 cannot occur.

We have shown that the formula is initially true, and that the only transitions that can falsify the formula can never occur. Hence those that do occur preserve the truth of the formula. □

Formula 3.3 is exactly the statement of the mutual exclusion property so the theorem has been proved. □

Unfortunately, the program can deadlock after just a few instructions if the interleaving executes one instruction from each process alternately.

1. P1 assigns 0 to C1.
2. P2 assigns 0 to C2.
3. P1 tests C2 and remains in the loop.
4. P2 tests C1 and remains in the loop.

Now the program will interleave tests all of which fail. Thus we have a situation where a set of processes (both of them) wish to enter the critical section, but no process will ever succeed.

3.5   Fourth Attempt

In the third attempt, when a Pi sets the variable Ci to 0, it not only indicates its intention to enter its critical section, but also *insists* on its right to do so. This can cause deadlock if both processes simultaneously insist on entering their critical sections.

The fourth attempt (Figure 3.5) attempts to remedy the problem by requiring a process to give up its intention to enter its critical section if it discovers that a state of contention with the other process exists. The sequence of assignments to the same variable C1:=1; C1:=0 is meaningful in a concurrent program, unlike a sequential program. Since we allow arbitrary interleaving of instructions from the two processes, P2 may be allowed to execute an arbitrary number of instructions between the two assignments to C1. In this case, when P1 relinquishes the attempt to enter the critical section by resetting C1 to 1, P2 may now execute the loop once more and succeed in entering the critical section.

This solution satisfies the mutual exclusion property for exactly the same reasons that the third attempt did. The transition to the critical section is made only if the variable in the other process is 1 and simple invariants describe exactly when this occurs. However, this solution suffers from two defects: individual starvation is possible, as well as a form of deadlock known as *livelock*. Recall that deadlock means that a set of processes wishes to enter their critical sections, but no process can succeed. In a deadlocked computation, there is *no* possible execution sequence which succeeds. In a livelocked computation, there are successful computations, but it is also possible to describe one or more execution sequences in which no process ever enters its critical section.

Theorem 3.5.1 *A process can be starved.*

Proof: Remember that arbitrary interleavings are possible. Between the two assignments to the variable C2, P1 can complete a full cycle of its outer loop and make another attempt to enter its critical section just as P2 makes another attempt.

1. P1 sets C1 to 0.
2. P2 sets C2 to 0.
3. P2 checks C1 and then resets C2 to 1.
4. P1 completes a full cycle:

```
                C1, C2: Integer range 0..1 := 1;

            task body P1 is
            begin
              loop
                Non_Critical_Section_1;
                C1 := 0;
                loop
                  exit when C2 = 1;
                  C1 := 1;
                  C1 := 0;
                end loop;
                Critical_Section_1;
                C1 := 1;
              end loop;
            end P1;

            task body P2 is
            begin
              loop
                Non_Critical_Section_2;
                C2 := 0;
                loop
                  exit when C1 = 1;
                  C2 := 1;
                  C2 := 0;
                end loop;
                Critical_Section_2;
                C2 := 1;
              end loop;
            end P2;
```

Figure 3.5 Fourth attempt

- Checks C2.
- Enters critical section.
- Resets C1.
- Executes non-critical section.
- Sets C1 to 0.

5. P2 sets C2 to 0.

We have now returned to the state described in line 3. The same steps can be repeated indefinitely, so it is possible to describe an execution sequence in which P1 enters its critical section infinitely often (so obviously this does not describe a deadlocked computation), but P2 remains indefinitely in its pre-protocol. □

Theorem 3.5.2 *The solution can livelock.*

Proof: Consider an execution sequence which perfectly alternates instructions of the two processes:

1. P1 sets C1 to 0.
2. P2 sets C2 to 0.
3. P1 checks C2 and remains in the loop.
4. P2 checks C1 and remains in the loop.
5. P1 resets C1 to 1.
6. P2 resets C2 to 1.
7. P1 sets C1 to 0.
8. P2 sets C2 to 0.
9. P1 checks C2 and remains in the loop.
10. P2 checks C1 and remains in the loop.

This execution sequence can be continued indefinitely. Thus we have the situation that defines deadlock: two processes wishing to enter their critical section, but none succeeding. However, the slightest deviation from the sequence described will allow one of the processes to enter its critical section. Thus we classify the problem as livelock rather than deadlock. □

It should be clear that the mutual exclusion property and the absence of deadlock are critical correctness requirements that must always be met in a real system. Livelock and starvation may be acceptable if the amount of contention is low so that the probability of these problems is negligible. A system designer must balance the probability and possible effects of these problems against the complexity of a more sophisticated algorithm which does not suffer from them.

3.6   Dekker's Algorithm

Dekker's algorithm (Figure 3.6) is a combination of the first and fourth attempted solutions. Recall that in the first solution we explicitly passed the right to enter the critical section between the processes. Unfortunately, this caused the processes to be too closely coupled and prevented correct behavior in the absence of contention. In the fourth solution, each process had its own variable which prevented problems in the absence of contention, but in the presence of contention neither process had the right to insist on entering its critical section.

Dekker's algorithm is like the fourth attempted solution, except that the right to *insist* is explicitly passed between the processes. The individual variables in each process will ensure mutual exclusion, but upon detecting contention, a process, say P1, will consult an additional global variable Turn to see if it is its turn to insist upon entering its critical section. If not, it will reset C1 and defer to P2, waiting on Turn. When the P2 completes its critical section, it will change Turn to 1, freeing P1. Even if P2 immediately made other requests to enter the critical section, it will be blocked by Turn once P1 re-issued its request.

Dekker's algorithm is correct: it satisfies the mutual exclusion property, it does not deadlock, neither process can be starved and in the absence of contention a process can enter its critical section immediately. The proofs are similar to those

```
        C1, C2: Integer range 0..1 := 1;
        Turn:   Integer range 1..2 := 1;
     task body P1 is
     begin
      loop
         Non_Critical_Section_1;
         C1 := 0;
         loop                             --------------------
   i1:    exit when C2 = 1;               -- insisting loop
   i2:    if Turn = 2 then                -- when Turn /= 2
              C1 := 1;
              loop exit when Turn = 1; end loop;
              C1 := 0;
           end if;
         end loop;                        --------------------
         Critical_Section_1;
         C1 := 1;
         Turn := 2;
      end loop;
     end P1;


     task body P2 is
     begin
       loop
         Non_Critical_Section_2;
         C2 := 0;
         loop                             --------------------
           exit when C1 = 1;              -- insisting loop
           if Turn = 1 then               -- when Turn /= 1
              C2 := 1;
              loop exit when Turn = 2; end loop;
              C2 := 0;
           end loop;                      --------------------
         Critical_Section_2;
         C2 := 1;
         Turn = 1;
       end loop;
     end P2;
```

Figure 3.6 Dekker's algorithm

of the previous attempts except for the proof of absence of starvation which we now proceed to do in some detail.

The statement we want to prove is that if P1 begins to execute its pre-protocol then *eventually* it will enter its critical section. A symmetric proof will show absence of starvation for P2. Unlike mutual exclusion which is a property that is *expressed* in terms of the location counters of both processes ($\neg at(d1 \land d2)$), absence of starvation can be expressed in terms of the location counters of P1 only. We are going to prove the theorem without using formulas that involve location counters of both processes.

We first prove two 'commitments'. These are theorems on the values of the global variables. They state that under certain assumptions on the behavior of the global variables, we can conclude that eventually something is true of another global variable. The theorems will be proved using only arguments on the structure of P2. Once we have proved that P2 is 'committed' to behave in some manner, we will prove that P1 cannot be starved. The advantage of this type of proof is that it is more elementary, since we have only to inspect the code of one process at a time. In addition, it would presumably be possible to replace the code of P2 by any other program that promised to behave as required by the commitments.

Theorem 3.6.1 *(Commitment 1)*

$$\Box C1 = 0 \wedge \Box Turn = 1 \supset \Diamond \Box C2 = 1$$

In words, if C1 *is held at* 0 *and* Turn *at* 1 *then eventually* C2 *is held at* 1.

Proof: The intended interpretation is that if P1 insists on entering its critical section then eventually C2 will defer.

Either P2 halts in its non-critical section, or P2 must progress through its protocols and/or critical section. In the first case, C2 is obviously held at 1. In the second case, C2 must eventually loop indefinitely in the inner loop on Turn. Note carefully how we are using the antecedents in the formula. Since C1 and Turn *always* have a certain value, no matter what the future interleaving of instructions from the processes, P2 is constrained to follow certain branches of each test. If the antecedent only said $\Diamond C1 = 0$ or even $\Box \Diamond C1 = 0$ (which means infinitely often $C1 = 0$), we could not make this claim because the interleaving could maliciously choose to make P2 check C1 when its value was not 0. $\Box$

Theorem 3.6.2 *(Commitment 2)*

$$\Box C1 = 1 \wedge \Box Turn = 2 \supset \Diamond Turn = 1$$

In words, if C1 *is held at* 1 *and* Turn *at* 2 *then eventually* $Turn = 1$.

Proof: The intended interpretation is that if it is P2's turn to insist, eventually it will return the right to insist to P1. Do not worry about the apparent contradiction between the antecedent and the consequent concerning the value of Turn. We will use this theorem to deduce that if $\Box C1 = 1$ then indeed $\Box Turn = 2$ is not true.

This statement can be proved only under the assumption that P2 does not halt in its non-critical section. The modifications needed for that special case are simple but tedious and have been left to an exercise.

Again, the formulas in the antecedent constrain P2 to take branches in each test that lead it necessarily to its critical section. Upon exiting the critical section, P2 sets Turn to 1. Note that Turn need not be held at 1 because P1 could quickly enter its critical section and set it to 2. $\Box$

Theorem 3.6.3 *If* P1 *enters its pre-protocol, then eventually it will enter its critical section.*

Proof: We will assume that P1 does not enter its critical section and derive a contradiction.

1. $\Box Turn = 2 \supset \Diamond\Box C1 = 1$. Under the assumption that P1 does not enter its critical section, it will not exit when C2=1. Thus it must follow the other branch and then loop indefinitely in the inner loop on Turn. By the invariant relating C1 to P1's location counter, C1 is held at 1.

2. $\Box Turn = 2 \supset \Diamond Turn = 1$. Commitment 2 (3.6.2) and line 1.

3. $\neg\Box Turn = 2 \supset \Diamond Turn = 1$. If Turn is not always 2, eventually it must have some other value. From the atomic operations and the program text, this value must be 1.

4. $\Diamond Turn = 1$. Elementary propositional calculus. If p implies q and so does $\neg p$, then q is true in any case.

5. $\Diamond\Box Turn = 1$. Once $Turn = 1$, the only way that it can change is for P1 to execute its critical section and then assign 2 to Turn. But we are assuming that P1 is currently in its pre-protocol and does not enter its critical section.

6. $\Diamond\Box(at(i1) \lor at(i2))$. If Turn is held at 1 and P1 does not enter its critical section, then we have now constrained P1 to branches that cause it to loop indefinitely in its insisting loop.

7. $\Diamond\Box C1 = 0$. If P1 loops indefinitely in its insisting loop, by the invariant on C1, the value of C1 is held at 0.

8. $\Diamond\Box C2 = 1$. Lines 5 and 7 are the antecedents of commitment 1 (3.6.1), so we can conclude the consequent of that formula.

But now we have a contradiction because P1 cannot loop in its insisting loop (line 6) if the value of C2 is held at 1 (line 8). Thus we conclude that the assumption that P1 never enters its critical section is false. □

3.7 Mutual Exclusion for N Processes

Dekker's algorithm solves the mutual exclusion problem for two processes. It is possible to construct algorithms for mutual exclusion for N processes, where N is arbitrary. These solutions are not often used in practice because they are relatively complicated and in the next section we will see that simple solutions are possible with hardware assistance. Nevertheless, we will give one example of such a solution – the bakery algorithm. This algorithm is not very practical as presented, but the basic idea has been used in more advanced algorithms. In addition, it will allow us to explore an interesting variant of the common memory model of concurrency.

In the bakery algorithm, a process wishing to enter its critical section is required to take a numbered ticket whose value is greater than the values of all the outstanding tickets. Then it waits until its ticket has the lowest value. The name of the algorithm comes from a similar situation in a bakery which has a ticket dispenser at the entrance. Customers are served in order of ascending ticket numbers.

The advantage this scheme is that there need be no variable which is both read and written by more than one process (like the variable Turn in Dekker's algorithm). Thus the bakery algorithm can be implemented on a wider range of architectures than those algorithms requiring atomic load and store to the same global variables. At the end of the section, we shall see that the bakery algorithm remains correct under an even weaker model of access to global variables.

Before looking at the full bakery algorithm, let us examine a simplified version for two processes (Figure 3.7). As promised, $N1$ is only assigned to in P1 and similarly for $N2$.

```
N1, N2: Integer := 0;

task body P1 is
begin
  loop
a1:    Non_Critical_Section_1;
b1:    N1 := 1;
c1:    N1 := N2 + 1;
d1:    loop exit when N2 = 0 or N1 <= N2; end loop;
e1:    Critical_Section_1;
f1:    N1 := 0;
  end loop;
end P1;

task body P2 is
begin
  loop
a2:    Non_Critical_Section_2;
b2:    N2 := 1;
c2:    N2 := N1 + 1;
d2:    loop exit when N1 = 0 or N2 < N1; end loop;
e2:    Critical_Section_2;
f2:    N2 := 0;
  end loop;
end P2;
```

Figure 3.7 Simplified bakery algorithm

Theorem 3.7.1 *The algorithm satisfies the mutual exclusion property.*

Proof: We will show that the following formulas are invariant:

$$N1 = 0 \equiv at(a1) \vee at(b1) \tag{3.4}$$
$$N2 = 0 \equiv at(a2) \vee at(b2) \tag{3.5}$$

$$at(e1) \supset (at(c2) \lor N2 = 0 \lor N1 \leq N2) \qquad (3.6)$$
$$at(e2) \supset (at(c1) \lor N1 = 0 \lor N2 < N1) \qquad (3.7)$$

Then if $at(e1) \land at(e2)$, we can deduce from the above formulas that $N1 \leq N2 \land N2 < N1$ which is clearly impossible.

Formulas 3.4 and 3.5 are trivial to prove and 3.7 follows by symmetry from 3.6.

Formula 3.6 is trivially true initially. All transitions in P1, except for $d1 \rightarrow e1$, trivially preserve the truth of 3.6 because $at(e1)$ is false and $false \supset p$ is always true. In the case of that transition, the condition on the loop ensures that the consequent is true.

Can a transition in P2 falsify the formula?

1. $a2 \rightarrow b2$, $d2 \rightarrow d2$, $d2 \rightarrow e2$ and $e2 \rightarrow f2$ trivially preserve the truth of the invariant because they do not assign to either variable nor do they affect the truth of $at(c2)$.
2. $b2 \rightarrow c2$ makes $at(c2)$ true.
3. $c2 \rightarrow d2$ makes $N1 \leq N2$ true.
4. $f2 \rightarrow a2$ makes $N2 = 0$ true. $\square$

The proofs of the other correctness properties (freedom from deadlock and starvation, behavior under contention) are left as exercises.

The bakery algorithm for N processes is shown in Figure 3.8. Each process chooses a number that is greater than the maximum of all outstanding ticket numbers. The array *choosing* is used as a flag to indicate to other processes that a process is in the act of choosing a ticket number. A process is allowed to enter its critical section when it has a lower ticket number than all other processes. In case of a tie in comparing ticket numbers, the lower numbered process is arbitrarily given precedence.

Theorem 3.7.2 *The bakery algorithm satisfies the mutual exclusion property.*

Proof: Assume Pi entered its critical section and then Pk entered its critical section. Before it entered its critical section, there was a last time Pi read the value of Choosing(k) and found it zero (to exit the loop $l1$), and a last time Pi read the value of Number(k) and succeeded in exiting the loop $l2$. Similarly, before Pk entered its critical section, there was a last time when it executed the three statements involved in taking a ticket.

Denoting by $read(v)$ and $write(v)$ these last times that a variable v was accessed, we have the following inequalities which are true because each process by itself is a sequential process: (3.8) describes the relations among times of instruction execution in Pi and similarly for (3.9) and Pk:[1]

$$write(N(i)) < read(C(k) = 0) < read(N(k)) \qquad (3.8)$$
$$write(C(k) := 1) < read(N(i)) < write(N(k)) < write(C(k) := 0) \qquad (3.9)$$

---

[1] We have contracted the notation and used just the first letter of each variable.

```
Choosing: array(1..N) of Integer := (others => 0);
Number:   array(1..N) of Integer := (others => 0);

task body Pi is
  I: constant Integer := ... ; -- Task id
begin
  loop
    Non_Critical_Section_I;
    Choosing(I) := 1;
    Number(I)   := 1 + max(Number);
    Choosing(I) := 0;
    for J in 1..N loop
      if J /= I then
l1:     loop exit when Choosing(J) = 0; end loop;
l2:     loop
          exit when
            Number(J) = 0 or
            Number(I) < Number(J) or
            (Number(I) = Number(J) and I < J);
        end loop;
      end if;
    end loop;
    Critical_Section_I;
    Number(I) := 0;
  end loop;
end Pi;
```

Figure 3.8 Bakery algorithm

Now in order that Choosing(k) have a zero value so that Pi can leave the loop, it must have been read either before the 1 was written, or after the 0 was written following the choice of a ticket by Pk. So there are two cases to consider.

$$read(C(k) = 0) < write(C(k) := 1) \tag{3.10}$$

$$write(C(k) := 0) < read(C(k) = 0) \tag{3.11}$$

Case 1: Combining the formulas (3.8 and 3.9) derived from the sequential behavior of the program with the formula (3.10) defining this case we get:

$$write(N(i)) < read(C(k) = 0) < write(C(k) := 1) < read(N(i)) \tag{3.12}$$

From (3.12) and (3.9), Pk read $N(i)$ and used it to compute $N(k)$ after Pi has chosen it current ticket number, so $N(k)$ will larger than $N(i)$. Thus Pk cannot enter its critical section as long as Pi remains in its critical section and does not assign again to $N(i)$.

Case 2: Combining the sequential formulas with (3.11) we get:

$$write(N(k)) < write(C(k) := 0) < read(C(k) = 0) < read(N(k)) \tag{3.13}$$

Pi read the current value $N(k)$ and then entered its critical section, proving that $N(i) < N(k)$ and thus Pk will not enter its critical section. □

Let us now weaken the common memory model. Rather than assume that simultaneous reads and writes to a memory location are modeled as an arbitrary interleaving of the two instructions, we allow the read to return *any* value in its range though the write is assumed to execute correctly! If there is no contention for the variable, all instructions must execute correctly.

In case 1, $write(N(k))$ in Pk and $read(N(k))$ in Pi may be executed simultaneously. This may cause Pi not to enter its critical section if it mistakenly read a value for $N(k)$ that is too small. However, Pk will correctly execute the write to $N(k)$ of a larger value than $N(i)$. On the next cycle through the loop, Pi will read the correct value and enter the critical section. Mutual exclusion is preserved and the simultaneous read and write only caused a short delay in one process.

Despite the elegance of the bakery algorithm it is not practical for two reasons. Firstly, the ticket numbers will be unbounded if some process is always in the critical section. Secondly, even in the absence of contention, each process must query every other process for the value of its ticket number (and in this version also for the value of *choosing*). This can be very inefficient as the number of processes increases. Thus we abandon this model for higher level models of concurrency.

3.8 Hardware-Assisted Mutual Exclusion

Under a model which can interleave individual load and store instructions, we found that it was difficult to achieve mutual exclusion. The difficulty disappears if a load and a store are allowed in a single atomic instruction.

One example is the test and set instruction. It is equivalent to the two instructions in Figure 3.9 with no interleaving allowed between them. C is a global

```
Li := C;
C  := 1;
```

Figure 3.9 Test and set instruction

variable with initial value 0 which is accessible to all processes. Li is a variable local to process Pi. The mutual exclusion problem for N processes can now be solved very easily as shown in Figure 3.10. We leave it as an exercise to prove that this solution satisfies the mutual exclusion property.

Another instruction is Exchange(A,B) which is equivalent to an atomic execution of the statements in Figure 3.11. Mutual exclusion is solved as shown in Figure 3.12 where C is a global variable initialized to 1. Here too, proofs of correctness are left as exercises.

3.9 Further Reading

The attempts leading up to Dekker's algorithm are taken from one of the earliest works on concurrent programming [Dij68]. A shorter algorithm is given in [Pet81]. The bakery algorithm is from [Lam74]. Raynal's book [Ray86] is a compilation of mutual exclusion algorithms.

```
task body Pi is
  Li: Integer range 0..1;
begin
  loop
    Non_Critical_Section_i;
    loop
      Test_and_Set(Li);
      exit when Li=0;
    end loop;
    Critical_Section_i;
    C := 0;
  end loop;
end Pi;
```

Figure 3.10 Mutual exclusion with Test_and_Set

```
Temp := A;
A    := B;
B    := Temp;
```

Figure 3.11 Exchange instruction

An algorithm by Peterson [Pet83] solves mutual exclusion for N processes using variables taking a bounded number of values (four), unlike the unbounded values of the bakery algorithm. An algorithm by Lamport [Lam87] solves the mutual exclusion problem with only five accesses to global variables per entry into the critical section in the absence of contention. Compare that to the bakery algorithm which queries every one of the other $N-1$ processes at least three times even in the absence of contention.

```
task body Pi is
  Li: Integer range 0..1 := 0;
begin
  loop
    Non_Critical_Section_i;
    loop
      Exchange(C,Li);
      exit when Li=1;
    end loop;
    Critical_Section_i;
    Exchange(C,Li);
  end loop;
end Pi;
```

Figure 3.12 Mutual exclusion with Exchange

3.10   Exercises

1. Prove the mutual exclusion property for the First Attempt. (*Hint*: The invariant is: $(at(CS1) \supset Turn = 1) \wedge (at(CS2) \supset Turn = 2)$.)

2. Prove the mutual exclusion property of Dekker's algorithm.

3. Prove the correctness properties for test and set.

4. Solve the mutual exclusion problem using Exchange(A,B). Prove the correctness of the solution.

5. Prove that the values of the ticket numbers in the bakery algorithm can be unbounded.

6. Prove that the statements Ni:=1 in the simplified bakery algorithm cannot be removed.

7. Prove that the simplified bakery algorithm is not correct under the weaker model that allows simultaneous load and store.

8. Modify the proof of the liveness of Dekker's algorithm to include the possibility that P2 is allowed to halt in its non-critical section. (*Hint*: The consequent of Commitment 2 becomes $\Diamond Turn = 1 \vee \Diamond \Box C2 = 1$. But most of the proof of Theorem 3.6.3 is devoted to using $\Diamond Turn = 1$ to prove $\Diamond \Box C2 = 1$).

9. Prove the correctness of Peterson's algorithm (Figure 3.13). (*Hint*: For liveness, prove the sequence of formulas in Figure 3.14 and show that the last two are contradictory).

```
C1, C2: Integer range 0..1 := 0;
Last:   Integer range 1..2 := 1;

task body P1 is
begin
  loop
a1: Non_Critical_Section_1;
b1: C1 := 1;
c1: Last := 1;
d1: loop exit when C2=0 or Last /= 1; end loop;
e1: Critical_Section_1;
f1: C1 := 0;
  end loop;
end P1;

task body P2 is
begin
  loop
a2: Non_Critical_Section_1;
b2: C2 := 1;
c2: Last := 2;
d2: loop exit when C1=0 or Last /= 2; end loop;
e2: Critical_Section_2;
f2: C2 := 0;
  end loop;
end P2;
```

Figure 3.13 Peterson's algorithm for mutual exclusion

1. $\Box(C2 = 0) \vee \Diamond(Last = 2)$

2. $at(d1) \wedge \neg\Diamond at(e1) \supset \Box\Diamond(C2 = 1)$

3. $at(d1) \wedge \neg\Diamond at(e1) \supset \Diamond(Last = 2)$

4. $at(d1) \wedge \neg\Diamond at(e1) \supset \Diamond\Box(Last = 2)$

5. $at(d1) \wedge \neg\Diamond at(e1) \supset \Box\Diamond(Last = 1)$

Figure 3.14 Proof of liveness of Peterson's algorithm

Chapter 4

Semaphores

4.1 Introduction

The algorithms in the previous chapter can be run on a *bare machine*. That is, they use only the machine language instructions that the computer provides. Though bare-machine instructions can be used to implement correct solutions to mutual exclusion and other concurrent programming problems, they are too low level to be efficient and reliable. In this chapter, we will study the *semaphore* which provides a concurrent programming primitive on a higher level than machine instructions. Semaphores are usually implemented by an underlying operating system, but for now we will investigate them by defining the required behavior and assuming that this behavior can be efficiently implemented.

A semaphore is an integer-valued variable which can take only non-negative values. Exactly two operations are defined on a semaphore S:

Wait(S) If $S > 0$ then $S := S - 1$ else suspend the execution of this process. The process is said to be suspended *on* the semaphore S.

Signal(S) If there are processes that have been suspended on this semaphore, wake one of them else $S := S + 1$.

The semaphore has the following properties:

1. `Wait(S)` and `Signal(S)` are atomic instructions.[1] In particular, no instructions can be interleaved between the test that $S > 0$ and the decrement of S or the suspension of the calling process.

2. A semaphore must be given a non-negative initial value.

3. The `Signal(S)` operation must waken one of the suspended processes. The definition does *not* specify which process will be awakened.

A semaphore which can take any non-negative value is called a *general semaphore*. A semaphore which takes only the values 0 and 1 is called a *binary semaphore* in which case `Signal(S)` is defined by: if ... else $S := 1$.

---

[1] The original notation is P(S) for `Wait(S)` and V(S) for `Signal(S)`, the letters P and V taken from corresponding words in Dutch.

4.2   Semaphore Invariants

A semaphore satisfies the following invariants:

$$S \geq 0 \tag{4.1}$$

$$S = S0 + \#Signals - \#Waits \tag{4.2}$$

where $S0$ is the initial value of the semaphore, $\#Signals$ is the number of signals executed on S, and $\#Waits$ is the number of completed waits executed on S. These invariants follow directly from the definition of semaphores, i.e. if you write a program and one of these formulas is not invariant, you have been given a defective implementation of semaphores.

The only non-trivial part to prove is the case of a signal which wakes a suspended process. But then $\#Signals$ and $\#Waits$ both increase by one so their difference remains invariant as does the value of S.

In the next section we give a solution to the mutual exclusion problem using semaphores and prove its correctness by appealing to the semaphore invariants.

4.3   Mutual Exclusion

Figure 4.1 is a solution to the mutual exclusion problem for two processes using semaphores. A process that wishes to enter its critical section, say P1, executes a pre-protocol that consists only of the Wait(S) instruction. If $S = 1$ then S can be decremented and P1 enters its critical section. When P1 exits its critical section

```
S: Semaphore := 1;

task body P1 is
begin
  loop
    Non_Critical_Section_1;
    Wait(S);
    Critical_Section_1;
    Signal(S);
  end loop;
end P1;

task body P2 is
begin
  loop
    Non_Critical_Section_2;
    Wait(S);
    Critical_Section_2;
    Signal(S);
  end loop;
end P2;
```

Figure 4.1 Mutual exclusion with semaphores

and executes the post-protocol consisting only of the `Signal(S)` instruction, the value S will once more be 1. However, if P2 attempts to enter its critical section before P1 has left, $S = 0$ and P2 will suspend on S. When P1 finally leaves, the `Signal(S)` will wake P2.

The solution is similar to the second attempt of the previous chapter, except that the atomic implementation of the semaphore instruction prevents interleaving between the test of S and the assignment to S. It differs from the test and set instruction in that a process suspended on a semaphore no longer executes instructions checking variables in a busy-wait loop.

Theorem 4.3.1 *The mutual exclusion property is satisfied.*

Proof: Let $\#CS$ be the number of processes in their critical sections. We will prove that
$$\#CS + S = 1 \tag{4.3}$$
is invariant. Since $S \geq 0$ by invariant (4.1), simple arithmetic shows that $\#CS \leq 1$ which proves the mutual exclusion property.

To prove that (4.3) is invariant, we use the semaphore invariant (4.2).

1. $\#CS = \#Wait(S) - \#Signal(S)$. An invariant easily proven from the program text.
2. $S = 1 + \#Signal(S) - \#Wait(S)$. The semaphore invariant.
3. $S = 1 - \#CS$. From (1) and (2).
4. $\#CS + S = 1$. Immediate from (3). $\square$

Theorem 4.3.2 *The program cannot deadlock.*

Proof: For the program to deadlock, both process must be suspended on `Wait(S)`. Then $S = 0$ because they are suspended and $\#CS = 0$ since neither is in the critical section. By the critical section invariant (4.3), $0 + 0 = 1$ which is impossible. $\square$

Theorem 4.3.3 *There is no individual starvation.*

Proof: If P1 is suspended, the semaphore must be 0. By the semaphore invariant, P2 is in the critical section. When P2 exits the critical section, it will execute `Signal(S)` which will wake some process suspended on S. Since P1 is the only process suspended on S, it will be awakened and enter its critical section. $\square$

Finally, it should be obvious that in the absence of contention, $S = 1$ and no single process will be delayed.

4.4 Semaphore Definitions

There are many definitions of semaphores in the literature. It is important to be able to distinguish between the various definitions because the correctness of a program will depend on the exact definition used.

Blocked-set semaphore A signaling process awakens *one* of the suspended processes. This is the semaphore we have been using.

- `Wait(S)`: If $S > 0$ then $S := S - 1$ else suspend the execution of this process.

- `Signal(S)`: If there are processes that have been suspended on this semaphore, wake one of them else $S := S + 1$.

Blocked-queue semaphore The suspended processes are kept on a FIFO queue and awakened in the same order that they were suspended.

- `Wait(S)`: If $S > 0$ then $S := S - 1$ else suspend the execution of this process. It is appended at the tail of a FIFO queue.

- `Signal(S)`: If there are processes that have been suspended on this semaphore, wake the process at the head of the queue else $S := S + 1$.

Busy-wait semaphore The value of S is tested in a busy-wait loop. The entire if-statement is executed as an atomic operation, but there may be interleaving between cycles of the loop.

- `Wait(S)`:
  ```
  loop
    if S > 0 then S := S-1; exit; end if;
  end loop;
  ```
- `Signal(S)`: S:=S+1.

Strongly-fair semaphore If the semaphore is signaled infinitely often, eventually every waiting process will complete the semaphore instruction (that is, if l is the location of the `Wait` instruction, eventually the instruction pointer of the process will be at l': the next location following the `Wait`).

- `Wait(S)`: $at(l) \wedge \Box \Diamond S > 0 \supset \Diamond at(l')$.

- `Signal(S)`: $S := S + 1$.

Weakly-fair semaphore If the semaphore is held at a value greater than zero, eventually every waiting process will complete the semaphore instruction.

- `Wait(S)`: $at(l) \wedge \Diamond \Box S > 0 \supset \Diamond at(l')$.

- `Signal(S)`: $S := S + 1$.

The blocked-set and blocked-queue definitions define a semaphore in terms of an underlying implementation that is able to maintain data structures of suspended processes and perform actions on the data struction such as adding and deleting processes.

The busy-wait semaphore also defines a semaphore in terms of an implementation, though such an implementation is rather inefficient and can only be considered in a distributed environment where the overhead of busy-wait might not be important.

The strongly-fair and weakly-fair semaphores (or *strong* and *weak* semaphores) are defined in terms of their abstract fairness behavior and not in terms of their implementation. If a strong semaphore gets a positive value infinitely often, eventually a process that executed Wait(S) will complete the execution of the instruction. A weak semaphore only promises completion of Wait(S) if the semaphore is held indefinitely at a positive value.

A busy-wait semaphore is an implementation of a weak semaphore. It is not a strong semaphore since it is possible that S could become positive and then return to zero exactly in the intervals between the time that the process checks S. On the other hand, the blocked queue semaphore is strong since any signal will wake a blocked process.

The correctness of the solution for mutual exclusion is affected by the definition chosen for the semaphores. All semaphores satisfy the semaphore invariants, of course, so the proof of the mutual exclusion property does not change. The proof of absence of deadlock is differs only in the details. The situation is different with starvation.

First note that although the solution was given for two processes, the algorithm and the proofs immediately generalize to N processes (Figure 4.2). For this

```
S: Semaphore := 1;

task body Pi is
begin
  loop
    Non_Critical_Section_i;
    Wait(S);
    Critical_Section_i;
    Signal(S);
  end loop;
end Pi;
```

Figure 4.2 Mutual exclusion for N processes

generalization, we can prove that the starvation property of the program depends on the semaphore definition chosen.

Theorem 4.4.1 *For a busy-wait semaphore, starvation is possible.*

Proof: Consider the following execution sequence:

1. P1 executes Wait(S) and enters its critical section.
2. P2 finds $S = 0$ and loops.
3. P1 completes an entire cycle consisting of post-protocol, non-critical section, pre-protocol and re-enters its critical section.
4. P2 finds $S = 0$ and loops.

This can be continued indefinitely causing starvation of P2. The interleaving is conspiring to allow P2 to check the value of S exactly when P1 is in its critical section. □

Theorem 4.4.2 *For a blocked-queue semaphore, starvation is impossible.*

Proof: Suppose P1 is blocked on S. Then there are *at most* $N - 1$ processes ahead of P1 on the queue for S. Thus P1 will enter its critical section after at most $N - 1$ more executions of Signal(S). □

Theorem 4.4.3 *For a blocked-set semaphore, starvation is possible for $N \geq 3$.*

Proof: For $N = 2$ we have shown that starvation is impossible. For $N \geq 3$, it is possible to construct an execution sequence where there will always be at least two processes blocked on S. For a blocked-set semaphore, Signal(S) is only required to wake one arbitrary process, so it can conspire to ignore one process causing starvation. The details of the construction are left as an exercise. □

4.5   Producer–Consumer Problem

The mutual exclusion problem is an abstraction of synchronization problems common in computer systems. Now we will look at an abstraction of communications problems called the *producer–consumer problem*. Two types of processes exist:

Producers By executing an internal procedure Produce, these processes create a data element which must then be sent to the consumers.

Consumers Upon receipt of a data element, these processes perform some computation in an internal procedure Consume.

For example, this models an application producing a listing that must be consumed by a printer process, as well as a keyboard handler producing a line of data that will be consumed by an application program. The discussion will be in terms of one producer process sending a data element to one consumer process. The generalization to multiple producers and/or multiple consumers is immediate.

Whenever a data element has to be sent from one process to another, an elementary solution is synchronous communication: when one process is ready to send and the other to receive, the data element is transferred. If more flexibility is required, a *buffer* is introduced in order to allow asynchronous communications. A buffer is a queue of data elements. The sending process *appends* a data element to the tail of the queue and the receiving process *removes* a data element from the head of a non-empty queue. The use of a buffer allows processes of similar average speeds to proceed smoothly in spite of differences in transient performance.

A familiar example is the type-ahead feature found in most interactive computer systems. The user may type several commands without waiting for the computer to complete the execution of the current command. It is possible to request six compilations and then concurrently go to lunch, which is better than entering a command every five minutes exactly. The computer is well utilized this way because it can start a second compilation immediately after finishing with the first one, rather than waiting for the user to notice that it has terminated and type in the next command.

It is important to understand that a buffer is of no use if the average speeds of the two processes are very different. To continue the example, there is no reason for a user to enter more commands than the computer can process in a single day. Conversely, if the commands are processed faster than the user can type, the buffer will remain empty.

An additional reason for using a buffer is to resolve a clash in the structure of data. A user types in characters one at a time but the computer processes complete commands. The buffer is also used to accumulate the characters typed by the user until a complete command can be submitted for processing.

4.6   Infinite Buffers

We begin the study of the producer–consumer problem with an implementation that assumes the existence of an infinite data structure, in this case an infinite array B that will store data of some type such as `Integer` (Figure 4.3). While

```
B: array(0..infinity) of Integer;
In_Ptr, Out_Ptr: Integer := 0;

task body Producer is
  I: Integer;
begin
  loop
    Produce(I);
    B(In_Ptr) := I;
    In_Ptr := In_Ptr + 1;
  end loop;
end Producer;

task body Consumer is
  I: Integer;
begin
  loop
    Wait until In_Ptr > Out_Ptr;
    I := B(Out_Ptr);
    Out_Ptr := Out_Ptr + 1;
    Consume(I);
  end loop;
end Consumer;
```

Figure 4.3 Producer–consumer with infinite buffer

obviously not practical, the infinite buffer leads naturally to techniques for programming finite buffers.

Two index variables In_Ptr and Out_Ptr indicate the next available position to place an element into the buffer and the oldest element which can be taken out of the buffer (see Figure 4.4).

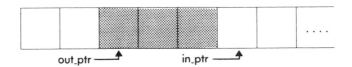

Figure 4.4 Indices in the infinite buffer

In_Ptr counts the number of elements placed in the buffer and Out_Ptr the number of elements removed. Thus $\#E = In\_Ptr - Out\_Ptr$ is the number of elements currently in the buffer and is never negative by the condition in the consumer. (Note that $In\_Ptr = Out\_Ptr$ indicates an empty buffer $\#E = 0$.) We have shown that the following equations are invariants:

$$\#E \geq 0 \tag{4.4}$$
$$\#E = 0 + In\_Ptr - Out\_Ptr \tag{4.5}$$

But these are precisely the same as equations (4.1) and (4.2) which define a semaphore! The producer–consumer problem, in particular the synchronization needed by the consumer, can be solved using a semaphore Elements that represents the number of elements in the buffer (Figure 4.5).

The semaphore Elements is explicitly counting the number of elements in the buffer. Elements is initialized to 0 representing the fact that the buffer is initially empty. The consumer executes Wait(Elements) which suspends if the number of elements in the buffer is zero. Finally we have to add a Signal(Elements) instruction to the producer. In the partial implementation of Figure 4.3, the consumer 'instantaneously' senses that $In\_Ptr > Out\_Ptr$. In the actual implementation, we have to physically inform the consumer whether the buffer is empty or not by signaling the semaphore.

4.7 Bounded Buffers

A practical buffer must be finite. There are two techniques used to bound the size of a buffer. The first is the *circular buffer* which is like the infinite buffer except that the index is computed modulo the length of the array (Figure 4.6). In addition to synchronization ensuring that the consumer does not try to remove an element from an empty buffer, we will have to introduce synchronization to ensure that the producer does not append to a full buffer.

The other method of bounding a buffer is to note that once data have been consumed from the low indices of the infinite buffer, that space is never used again, so we could move it to the high indices instead of asking for new array elements. This is done by allocating a *pool* of finite buffers (Figure 4.7). The producer is given a buffer to fill which is then passed to the consumer. When the consumer has removed all the elements from buffer, it is returned to the pool. Synchronization is needed to ensure that the consumer can be suspended while waiting for the next buffer from the producer and that the producer can be suspended if there

```
B: array(0..infinity) of Integer;
In_Ptr, Out_Ptr: Integer := 0;
Elements: Semaphore := 0;

task body Producer is
  I: Integer;
begin
  loop
    Produce(I);
    B(In_Ptr) := I;
    In_Ptr := In_Ptr + 1;
    Signal(Elements);
  end loop;
end Producer;

task body Consumer is
  I: Integer;
begin
  loop
    Wait(Elements);
    I := B(Out_Ptr);
    Out_Ptr := Out_Ptr + 1;
    Consume(I);
  end loop;
end Consumer;
```

Figure 4.5 Semaphore solution for infinite buffers

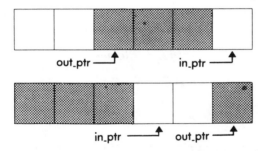

Figure 4.6 Circular buffer

are no free buffers in the pool. The circular buffer is very simple and efficient and is to be preferred in most cases. Examples of situations where a buffer pool would be more appropriate include:

- The producer or the consumer is a hardware controller that needs the data in sequential memory locations and cannot do modulo arithmetic.

- The amount of buffering needed changes with time. A communications system may need a large amount of buffer space to deal with a burst of activity on

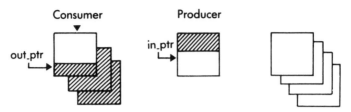

Figure 4.7 Pool of buffers

a line, but this can be reduced to almost nothing when the line is inactive. Memory utilization will be better if the buffers are shared among all the lines rather than allocating a maximal size circular buffer for each line.

- A circular buffer is a true global variable and certain architectures might find this inefficient to implement. A buffer from a pool can be copied. Also, it may be more efficient to pretend that each element created by the producer is its own buffer rather than copy the element into the circular buffer. This introduces a tight coupling between the design of the producer and the buffering scheme and should be avoided if possible.

Now we show how to program a circular buffer (Figure 4.8) and leave the buffer pool for a later chapter. Create a semaphore Spaces to count *empty* places in the buffer. When there is no more space the producer will suspend until the consumer removes an element and signals. The indices are incremented modulo N, the length of the buffer.

Theorem 4.7.1 *Let $\#E$ be the number of elements in the buffer. The following formulas are invariant at the beginning of each cycle of a loop:*

$$\#E = Elements \qquad\qquad (4.6)$$

$$\#E = N - Spaces \qquad\qquad (4.7)$$

Proof: Exercise. □

Theorem 4.7.2 *The program never removes an element from an empty buffer nor does it append one to a full buffer.*

Proof: Taking from an empty buffer means executing a cycle of the consumer loop when $\#E = 0$. By (4.6), *Elements* $= 0$ so the consumer will be suspended and not remove an element from the empty buffer. The proof for the full buffer is similar and left as an exercise. □

We also have to show that the elements are removed in the order they were appended but this proof involves techniques beyond the scope of the book.

Theorem 4.7.3 *The program cannot deadlock.*

```
B: array(0..N-1) of Integer;
In_Ptr, Out_Ptr: Integer := 0;
Elements: Semaphore := 0;
Spaces: Semaphore := N;

task body Producer is
  I: Integer;
begin
  loop
    Produce(I);
    Wait(Spaces);
    B(In_Ptr) := I;
    In_Ptr := (In_Ptr + 1) mod N;
    Signal(Elements);
  end loop;
end Producer;

task body Consumer is
  I: Integer;
begin
  loop
    Wait(Elements);
    I := B(Out_Ptr);
    Out_Ptr := (Out_Ptr + 1) mod N;
    Signal(Spaces);
    Consume(I);
  end loop;
end Consumer;
```

Figure 4.8 Semaphore solution for circular buffers

Proof: For deadlock, both processes are suspended on semaphores so *Spaces* = *Elements* = 0. By (4.6) and (4.7), $\#E = 0$ and $\#E = N - 0 = N$ which is impossible.[2] $\square$

Theorem 4.7.4 *There is no starvation of either process.*

Proof: Assume the producer is suspended on Wait(Spaces) indefinitely while the consumer executes an infinite number of cycles of its loop. But even a single cycle of the consumer loop signals the semaphore Spaces releasing the producer. Note that like in the mutual exclusion problem, this theorem depends on the number of processes and on the definition used for the semaphores. $\square$

---

[2] Impossible if $N > 0$. A buffer of zero length will cause deadlock!

4.8   Producer–Consumer with Binary Semaphores

The bounded buffer in the previous section was programmed using general semaphores which can take any non-negative value. In this section, we modify the
solution to use only binary semaphores. Not only is this useful if you have a system that supplies only binary semaphores, but it also demonstrates some pitfalls
that must be avoided when using these and similar primitives.

   In this solution (Figure 4.9), an explicit counter Count is used to keep track of
the number of elements in the buffer. The semaphore S protects this global variable from simultaneous access by the two processes and the semaphores Not_Empty
and Not_Full are used to block the producer and the consumer, respectively.

   Incrementing In_Ptr and Out_Ptr can be done outside the critical section,
because they are used only within a single task. The load and store of the element
in the buffer can also be done outside the critical section provided that the buffer
is modified before incrementing or decrementing Count. If not, the other process
could interleave statements between the update of Count and that of the buffer,
making assumptions based on the value of Count that are not true of the buffer
itself.

   The variables Local_Count are used to allow a process to test the value of
Count the last time it changed the value. This is needed because semaphores
have memory. That is, for each Signal, there must be a corresponding Wait.
Without the local variables (i.e. if we substitute Count for Local_Count in the
test statements), the following execution sequence would be possible:

1. The producer appends an element, sets Count to 1, and executes Signal
   (Not_Empty), so $Not\_Empty = 1$.

2. The consumer checks Count which is non-zero and does not execute Wait
   (Not_Empty). The consumer removes an element and sets Count to 0. The
   state of the computation now is that the buffer is empty, $Count = 0$ but
   $Not\_Empty = 1$.

3. The consumer re-enters its loop and since $Count = 0$, it will execute Wait
   (Not_Empty). Since $Not\_Empty = 1$, it will remove an element from an
   empty buffer which clearly is incorrect behavior.

The use of the local variable will cause the consumer to execute Wait(Not_Empty)
even though this is not strictly necessary since there are actually data in the buffer.

4.9   Further Reading

This chapter is also based on [Dij68]. Stark ([Sta82]) has formalized the various
definitions of semaphores and proved theorems that compare them on the mutual
exclusion problem.

```
        B: array(0..N-1) of Integer;
        In_Ptr, Out_Ptr, Count: Integer := 0;
        S: Binary_Semaphore := 1;
        Not_Empty, Not_Full: Binary_Semaphore := 0;

    task body Producer is
        I: Integer;
        Local_Count: Integer := 0;
    begin
        loop
            Produce(I);
            if Local_Count = N then Wait(Not_Full); end if;
            B(In_Ptr) := I;
            Wait(S);
            Count := Count + 1;
            Local_Count := Count;
            Signal(S);
            if Local_Count = 1 then Signal(Not_Empty); end if;
            In_Ptr := (In_Ptr + 1) mod N;
        end loop;
    end Producer;

    task body Consumer is
        I: Integer;
        Local_Count: Integer := 0;
    begin
        loop
            if Local_Count = 0 then Wait(Not_Empty); end if;
            I := B(Out_Ptr);
            Wait(S);
            Count := Count - 1;
            Local_Count := Count;
            Signal(S);
            if Local_Count = N-1 then Signal(Not_Full); end if;
            Out_Ptr := (Out_Ptr + 1) mod N;
            Consume(I);
        end loop;
    end Consumer;
```

Figure 4.9 Circular buffer with binary semaphores

4.10 Exercises

1. Prove freedom from deadlock in the solution of the mutual exclusion problem under all definitions of semaphores.

2. Complete the proof of Theorem 4.4.3.

3. Prove Theorem 4.7.1.

4. Complete the proof of Theorem 4.7.2.

5. What would happen if several producers and consumers tried to share a buffer using the algorithm in Figure 4.8? Modify the solution to cover this case.

6. In Figure 4.9, prove that the Count must not be modified before B.

7. Prove that Local_Count is needed in the producer as well as the consumer of Figure 4.9.

Chapter 5

Monitors

5.1 Introduction

The semaphore was introduced to provide a synchronization primitive that does not require busy waiting. Using semaphores, we have given solutions to common concurrent programming problems. However, the semaphore is still a low-level primitive because it is unstructured. If we were to build a large system using semaphores alone, the responsibility for the correct use of the semaphores is diffused among all the implementers of the system. If one of them forgets to call Signal(S) after a critical section, the program can deadlock and the cause of the failure will be difficult to isolate.

Monitors provide a structured concurrent programming primitive that concentrates the responsibility for correctness into a few modules. Monitors are a generalization of the monolithic monitor (or *kernel* or *supervisor*) found in operating systems. Critical sections such as allocation of I/O devices and memory, queuing requests for I/O, and so on, are centralized in a privileged program. Ordinary programs request *services* which are performed by the central monitor. These programs are run in a hardware mode that ensures that they cannot be interfered with by ordinary programs. Because of the separation between the system and its applications programs, it is usually clear who is at fault if the system crashes (though it may be extremely difficult to diagnose the exact reason).

The monitors discussed in this chapter are decentralized versions of the monolithic monitor. Rather then have one system program handle all requests for services involving shared devices or data structures, we can define a separate monitor for each object or related group of objects. Processes request services from the various monitors. If the same monitor is called by two processes, the implementation ensures that these are processed serially to preserve mutual exclusion. If different monitors are called, their executions can be interleaved.

The syntax of monitors is based on *encapsulating* items of data and the procedures that operate upon them in a single module. The interface to a monitor will consist of a set of procedures. These procedures operate on data that are hidden within the module. The difference between a monitor and an ordinary module such as an Ada package is that a monitor not only protects internal data from unrestricted access but also synchronizes calls to the interface procedures. The implementation ensures that the procedures are executed under mutual exclusion.

We will define a synchronization primitive that will allow a process to suspend itself if necessary. For example, in the producer–consumer problem:

- The only operations permitted on a buffer are append and remove an item.
- Append and remove exclude each other.
- A producer will suspend on a full buffer and a consumer on an empty buffer.

5.2   Producer–Consumer Problem

We will define the monitor construct in parallel with the solution of the producer–consumer problem (Figure 5.1).[1] Note that the monitor is not a process (Ada task), but a static module of data and procedure declarations. The actual producer and consumer processes have to be programmed separately (Figure 5.2).

```
monitor Producer_Consumer_Monitor is
  B: array(0..N-1) of Integer;
  In_Ptr, Out_Ptr: Integer := 0;
  Count: Integer := 0;
  Not_Full, Not_Empty: Condition;

procedure Append(I: in Integer) is
begin
    if Count = N then Wait(Not_Full); end if;
    B(In_Ptr) := I;
    In_Ptr := (In_Ptr + 1) mod N;
    Signal(Not_Empty);
end Append;

procedure Take(I: out Integer) is
begin
    if Count = 0 then Wait(Not_Empty); end if;
    I := B(Out_Ptr);
    Out_Ptr := (Out_Ptr + 1) mod N;
    Signal(Not_Full);
end Take;

end Producer_Consumer_Monitor;
```

Figure 5.1 Monitor for producer-consumer

Despite the syntactic similarity to an ordinary module (Ada package), the semantics of a monitor are different because only one process is allowed to execute

---

[1] Unlike most of the examples in this book, this one is not executable in Ada without modification. See Appendix B for details.

```
task body Producer is
  I: Integer;
begin
  loop
    Produce(I);
    Append(I);
  end loop;
end Producer;

task body Consumer is
  I: Integer;
begin
  loop
    Take(I);
    Consume(I);
  end loop;
end Consumer;
```

Figure 5.2 Producer and consumer processes

a monitor procedure at any time. In this case, the producer can be executing **Append** or the consumer **Take**, but not both. This ensures the mutual exclusion on the global variables, in particular, on the variable **Count** which is updated by both procedures.

The solution is more structured than the semaphore solution both because the data and procedures are encapsulated in a single module and because the mutual exclusion is provided automatically by the implementation. The producer and consumer processes see only abstract **Append** and **Take** operations and do not have to be concerned with correctly programming semaphores.

The solution that used binary semaphores, used three of them: S for mutual exclusion, and **Not_Empty** and **Not_Full** for synchronization. The mutual exclusion requirement is now satisfied by the definition of monitors. For synchronization, we define a structure called *condition variables*. A condition variable C has three operations defined upon it:[2]

Wait(C) The process that called the monitor procedure containing this statement is suspended on a FIFO queue associated with C. The mutual exclusion on the monitor is released.

Signal(C) If the queue for C is non-empty then wake the process at the head of the queue.

Non_Empty(C) A boolean function that returns true if the queue for C is non-empty.

The **Wait** operation allows a process to suspend itself. Conventionally, the name of the condition variable is chosen so that **Wait(C)** can be read: 'I am waiting

---

[2] We are using the same names *Wait* and *Signal* that were used for the semaphore operations, but there is no relation between the two primitives.

for C to occur', and `Signal(C)`: 'I am signaling that C has occurred'. However, a condition variable is just a signaling device, unlike a general semaphore which has a counter associated with it, so it is the responsibility of the programmer to ensure that the condition defined by C has actually occurred.

`Wait(C)` releases the mutual exclusion on the monitor, so that other processes can enter (and presumably help establish the condition required by C). `Signal(C)` is *memoryless*, that is, if no process is suspended on the queue for C, the operation is ignored.

In the producer–consumer example, we use two condition variables:

Not_Empty Used by the consumer to suspend itself until the buffer is not empty.

Not_Full Used by the producer to suspend itself until the buffer is not full.

The definition of `Signal(C)` only requires it to wake the first process suspended on C. It does not require this process to actually be scheduled for execution. In fact, the problem is not simple for the following reason. Remember that the process executing `Signal(C)` is inside a monitor procedure. Since we cannot have two processes within a monitor, this seems to require that the awakened process remain suspended until the signaling process has exited the monitor. Then, perhaps, we could require that the awakened process have priority over other processes. But what would happen if the signaling process issued more than one signal?

The difficulty is more than a matter of finding and implementing a reasonable definition for the signal operation. Remember that a signal is issued when a process has determined that the condition required by the suspended process exists. If we allow execution of any instructions between the signal and the time that the awakened process is allowed to continue, we will have to verify that the condition continues to hold.

The problem can be demonstrated in the producer–consumer problem. Suppose that there were two consumer processes C1 and C2 and one producer process P1. C1 is suspended on Not_Empty, C2 has just called Take and P1 is about to execute `Signal(Not_Empty)`. P1 awakens C1 and the buffer is not empty, but if C2 is allowed to enter the monitor, it could make the buffer empty again before C1 has a chance to act. Once C2 leaves the buffer, C1 is allowed to continue and will incorrectly take a value from an empty buffer.

The solution is to require that an awakened process be scheduled for immediate execution after the signal instruction. This *immediate resumption requirement* simplifies the programming and verification of software that uses monitors. This takes care of the problem demonstrated in the previous paragraph by giving priority to awakened processes over those that have yet to enter the monitor. There remains the problem of defining the relative priority of the signaling process and the awakened process. The simplest solution is to require that a signal be the *last* instruction executed in the procedure in which it occurs. Then the execution of the signal can be considered to reschedule the awakened process.

There are several ways of avoiding this restriction on signals, but we will not discuss them in the text.

5.3   Emulation of Semaphores by Monitors

In this section and the next one, we will show how to emulate a semaphore using monitors and conversely. This will not only show that the two primitives are of similar power and expressibility, but will also show that the monitor is a higher-level abstraction than a semaphore because the emulation in one direction will be so much easier. These emulations can also be used to port a program from a system supplying one primitive to a system supplying the other one.

```
monitor Semaphore_Emulation is
  S: Integer := S0;
  Not_Zero: Condition;

  procedure Semaphore_Wait is
  begin
    if S=0 then Wait(Not_Zero); end if;
    S := S - 1;
  end Semaphore_Wait;

  procedure Semaphore_Signal is
  begin
    S := S + 1;
    Signal(Not_Zero);
  end Semaphore_Signal;
end monitor;
```

Figure 5.3 Emulation of semaphores by monitors

The monitor in Figure 5.3 emulates a semaphore. The variable S holds the value of the semaphore and is initialized to some non-negative value S0. (We could also have defined another procedure to initialize S.) The condition variable Not_Zero maintains the queue of processes waiting for the semaphore to be non-zero.

Theorem 5.3.1 *The semaphore invariants hold:*

$$S \geq 0 \tag{5.1}$$

$$S = S0 + \#waits - \#signals \tag{5.2}$$

Proof: As usual, the proof is by induction on the execution sequence. Since each monitor procedure is executed under mutual exclusion with no possibility of interleaving, we can relax the proof rules. It is sufficient to prove that the formulas are invariant in any interleaving where every execution of a monitor procedure is a single atomic instruction. The fact that the variables may temporarily have values that falsify the invariant may be ignored since no other process can see these values. Remember that a Wait(C) instruction is considered to cause a process to leave the monitor, so the invariants must be checked there too.

For (5.1), $S0$ is assumed non-negative, so (5.1) is initially true. The only transition that could falsify the formula is an execution of `Semaphore_Wait` with $S = 0$. In that case, `Wait(Non_Zero)` will suspend the process. It will be awakened only by an execution of `Signal(Non_Zero)`. But the previous statement in `Semaphore_Signal` increased the value of S to 1. By the immediate resumption requirement, $S = 1$ when it is decremented.

The proof of 5.2 is left as an exercise. □

This proves the safety properties required of an implementation of a semaphore. The emulation implements a block-queue semaphore because condition variables are defined to have FIFO queues and because the immediate resumption requirement ensures that there is no possibility of interleaving a third process between a signaling process and the process awakened from a suspend wait.

5.4   Emulation of Monitors by Semaphores

To emulate monitors using semaphores, we need a semaphore S to ensure mutual exclusion on the monitor procedures and one semaphore C_Semaphore for each condition variable. The semaphores will be assumed to be blocked-queue semaphores in order to implement the FIFO requirement of monitors. Otherwise, we would have to program explicitly a queue of blocked processes.

In addition, we need a counter for each condition variable because the meaning of `Signal(C)` depends on whether the queue is empty or not. But there is no way to discover this for a semaphore, so we will have to explicitly program the counter.

Each procedure in the monitor will have `Wait(S)` as its first instruction and `Signal(S)` as its last.[3]

Each occurrence of `Wait(C)` is translated to:

```
C_Count := C_Count + 1;
Signal(S);
Wait(C_Semaphore);
Wait(S);
C_Count := C_Count - 1;
```

The definition of `Wait(C)` requires that the mutual exclusion on the monitor be released by `Signal(S)`. Obviously, to avoid deadlock, this must be done before waiting for the condition.

Each occurrence of `Signal(C)` is translated to:

```
if C_Count > 0 then
  Signal(C_Semaphore);
end if;
```

However, this does not correctly emulate the immediate resumption requirement. Remember that we have assumed that a `Signal(C)` will be the last instruction in a procedure, so a `Signal(S)` will follow immediately:

---

[3] Be careful not to confuse waits and signals of the two primitives.

```
if C_Count > 0 then
   Signal(C_Semaphore);
end if;
Signal(S);
```

Signaling the condition semaphore will awaken the suspended process. But it is still possible to interleave instructions from a third process between `Wait` (`C_Semaphore`) and `Wait(S)`. This third process could execute `Wait(S)` before the awakened process and violate the immediate resumption requirement. A signal on a blocked-queue semaphore is only required to awaken the process at the head of the queue in preference to other suspend processes; it is not required to give it priority scheduling.

The solution is not to release the mutual exclusion on the monitor when signaling, but to let it remain in force and have the awakened process take upon itself the requirement for releasing mutual exclusion. The pair of instructions `Signal(C)` followed by the end of the monitor procedure is now translated:

```
if C_Counter > 0 then
   Signal(C_Semaphore);
else
   Signal(S);
end if;
```

and `Wait(C)` is simplified to:

```
C_Count := C_Count + 1;
Signal(S);
Wait(C_Semaphore);
C_Count := C_Count - 1;
```

5.5 The Problem of the Readers and the Writers

The problem of the readers and the writers is the next abstract problem in concurrent programming that we will solve. It is similar to the mutual exclusion problem in that several processes are competing for access to a critical section. In this problem, however, we divide the processes into two classes:

Readers Processes which are not required to exclude one another.

Writers Processes which are required to exclude every other process, readers and writers alike.

The problem is an abstraction of access to databases, where there is no danger in having several processes read concurrently, but writing or changing the data must be done under mutual exclusion to ensure consistency. The concept database must be understood in the widest possible sense – even a simple table describing the status of a disk drive or the arrangement of windows on a terminal screen can be considered a database that may need to be protected by some solution to the problem of the readers and the writers.

A process that wishes to read (write) calls monitor procedure `Start_Read` (`Start_Write`). Upon returning from the procedure, the process reads (writes) and then calls another monitor procedure `End_Read` (`End_Write`) to indicate to the monitor that it has terminated (Figure 5.4). Even before looking at the monitor itself, it should be clear that the start-procedures may cause a process to suspend but that the end-procedures will only signal.

```
task body Reader is
begin
  loop
    Start_Read;
    Read_the_Data;
    End_Read;
  end loop;
end Reader;

task body Writer is
begin
  loop
    Start_Write;
    Write_the_Data;
    End_Write;
  end loop;
end Writer;
```

Figure 5.4 Readers and writers

The monitor (Figure 5.5) has two status variables:

Readers A counter of the number of readers which have successfully passed Start_Read and are currently reading.

Writing A flag which is true when a process is writing.

There are two condition variables:

OK_to_Read to suspend readers.

OK_to_Write to suspend writers.

The general form of the monitor code is not difficult to follow. The variables Readers and Writing are incremented[4] in the start-procedures and decremented in the end-procedures. At the beginning of the start-procedures, a boolean expression is checked to see if the process should be suspended and at the end of the end-procedures, an expression is checked to see if some condition should be signaled. These expressions determine the behavior of the monitor.

A reader is suspended if some process is currently writing ($Writing$) or is some process is waiting to write ($Non\_Empty(OK\_to\_Write)$). The first condition is obviously required by the statement of the problem. The second condition is a decision to give the first suspended writer priority over waiting readers. On the other hand, the writer is suspended only if there are processes currently reading

---
[4] It is convenient to use the term 'increment' for the boolean variable too, where True is greater than False.

($Readers \neq 0$) or writing ($Writing$). `Start_Write` does not check the condition queues.

`End_Read` executes `Signal(OK_to_Write)` if there are no more readers. If there are suspended writers, one will be awakened and allowed to complete `Start_Write`. Otherwise, the operation does nothing and we return to the initial state. `End_Write` gives priority to the first suspended reader, if any, otherwise it wakes suspended writers, if any.

Finally, what is the function of `Signal(OK_to_Read)` in `Start_Read`? This statement performs a *cascaded wakeup* of the suspended readers. Upon termination of a writer, we gave priority to waking a suspended reader over a suspended writer. However, if one process is allowed to read, we might as well awaken them all. When the first reader completes `Start_Read`, it will signal the next reader and so on, until this cascade of signals wakes all the currently suspended readers.

What about readers that attempt to start reading during the cascaded wake-up? Will they have priority over suspended writers? By the immediate resumption requirement, the cascaded wakeup will run to completion before any new reader is allowed to commence execution of a monitor procedure. When the last `Signal(OK_to_Read)` is executed (and does nothing because the queue is empty), the monitor will be released and a new reader may enter. However, it is subject to the usual check that will cause it to suspend if there are waiting writers.

To summarize:

- If there are suspended writers, a new reader is required to wait until the termination of (at least) the first write.

- If there are suspended readers, they will (all) be released before the next write.

5.6   Correctness Proofs

This section contains proofs of the correctness of the solution to the problem of the readers and the writers given in the previous section.

Let R be the number of processes currently reading and W the number of processes currently writing. Then the following formulas are invariant:[5]

$$R = Readers \tag{5.3}$$

$$W > 0 \equiv Writing \tag{5.4}$$

$$Non\_Empty(OK\_to\_Read) \supset (Writing \vee Non\_Empty(OK\_to\_Write)) \tag{5.5}$$

$$Non\_Empty(OK\_to\_Write) \supset (Readers \neq 0 \vee Writing) \tag{5.6}$$

The proofs are left as exercises. They are similar to the proofs of the correctness of the semaphore invariants for the emulation of semaphores by monitors. Remember that monitor invariants are only required to hold outside the monitor

---

[5]   Note that `Writing` is a boolean variable so its value $Writing$ is a boolean expression which is either $True$ or $False$. Similarly for the boolean function `Non_Empty`.

```
monitor Reader_Writer_Monitor is
   Readers: Integer := 0;
   Writing: Boolean := False;
   OK_to_Read, OK_to_Write: Condition;

procedure Start_Read is
begin
   if Writing or Non_Empty(OK_to_Write) then
      Wait(OK_to_Read);
   end if;
   Readers := Readers + 1;
   Signal(OK_to_Read);
end Start_Read;

procedure End_Read is
begin
   Readers := Readers - 1;
   if Readers = 0 then Signal(OK_to_Write); end if;
end End_Read;

procedure Start_Write is
begin
   if Readers /= 0 or Writing then
      Wait(OK_to_Write);
   end if;
   Writing := True;
end Start_Write;

procedure End_Write is
begin
   Writing := False;
   if Non_Empty(OK_to_Read) then
      Signal(OK_to_Read);
   else
      Signal(OK_to_Write);
   end if;
end End_Write;
end Reader_Writer_Monitor;
```

Figure 5.5 Monitor for readers and writers

procedures themselves and that the immediate resumption requirement allows one to infer that what was true before executing a signal is true upon release of a wait.

Theorem 5.6.1 *(Safety property of the solution) The following formula is invariant:*

$$(R > 0 \supset W = 0) \land (W > 0 \supset (W = 1 \land R = 0)) \tag{5.7}$$

In words: if some process is reading, there are no writers and if there are writers, there is only one writer and, furthermore, there are no readers.

Proof: Formula 5.7 is initially true since $R = W = 0$. Assume that 5.7 is true and show that each transition preserves the truth of the formula. The formula can be falsified by falsifying either of its conjuncts, so it is sufficient to show that no transition can falsify either one or the other.

Case 1: First conjunct:

$$R > 0 \supset W = 0 \tag{5.8}$$

Suppose that both antecedent ($R > 0$) and consequent ($W = 0$) are true. Formula 5.8 could be falsified if a process began to write, which can only happen if it successfully completes Start_Write.

Subcase 1.1: The process enters Start_Write and successfully completes it. But we are assuming that $R > 0$ and by (5.3), $Readers > 0$. Thus the process cannot complete Start_Write, instead it will be suspended on Wait(OK_to_Write).

Subcase 1.2: The process was suspended on OK_to_Write and was awakened by a signal. As before, from $R > 0$ we can deduce that $Readers > 0$, so the signal in End_Read will not be executed. Since $W = 0$, there are no writers, so no writer will executed the signal in End_Write.

Case 2: As in case 1, but assume that both $R > 0$ and $W = 0$ are false and that a process begins to read causing only the antecedent to become true.

Subcase 2.1: $\neg W = 0$ implies $Writing$ by (5.4) so a process trying to execute Start_Read will be suspended.

Subcase 2.2: From $\neg R > 0$, we deduce that there are no readers, so no reader will execute the signal in Start_Read. Since (5.7) is assumed true, $\neg W = 0$ implies $W = 1$. Then Signal(OK_to_Read) in End_Write will be executed causing $R > 0$ to become true, but $W = 0$ will also become true. Thus it is impossible to falsify the antecedent alone.

Case 3: Second conjunct:

$$W > 0 \supset (W = 1 \wedge R = 0) \tag{5.9}$$

Assume that the antecedent and consequent are both true and that the consequent is falsified. This can happen if a second process begins to write or if some process begins to read. The proofs that this is impossible are similar to the previous cases and are left to the reader.

Case 4: As in case 3, but assume that the antecedent and consequent are false and that the antecedent alone becomes true. As in Subcase 2.2, to go from $\neg W > 0$ to $W > 0$ means that W was 0 and now is 1. Also, $R = 0$ is true by the code in Start_Write for the subcase of a process entering and successfully exiting the procedure. For the subcase of a writer being awakened, we leave it as an exercise using (5.6). □

Theorem 5.6.2 *No process is starved.*

Proof: We will prove that no process wishing to read is starved and leave the proof for writers as an exercise.

If a process P tries to execute Start_Read, there are three possible outcomes:

1. P successfully completes the execution of the procedure. In this case, there is no starvation.

2. P never enters the procedure. Every other process either completes a monitor procedure or is suspended, waiting for a condition which also frees the mutual exclusion on the monitor. Since there is are a finite number of processes, eventually P will be allowed to enter.[6] This case reduces to the other two.

3. P is suspended by Wait(OK_to_Read). This is the difficult case.

So suppose that P is enqueued on OK_to_Read. There are only a finite number of processes enqueued before P. We fill show that eventually Signal(OK_to_Read) must be executed. By (ordinary numerical) induction on the number of processes before P we can conclude that there is no starvation.

By invariant 5.5, *Writing* or *Non_Empty(OK_to_Write)*.

Case 1: Writing. By (5.4), $W > 0$. Eventually one of these writers (actually there is only one) must finish writing and execute End_Write. Since *Non_Empty (OK_to_Read)*, the writer must execute Signal(OK_to_Read).

Case 2: Non_Empty(OK_to_Write). By (5.6), *Readers* $\neq 0 \vee$ *Writing*. If *Writing*, then eventually a writer executes Signal(OK_to_Read) as in case 1. If *Readers* $\neq 0$, eventually they each execute End_Read. Since *Non_Empty (OK_to_Write)*, no new readers can complete Start_Read, so eventually the last reader executes Signal(OK_to_Write) in End_Read and this reduces to the previous cases. $\square$

5.7   Further Reading

Monitors were introduced by Hoare [Hoa74]. The verification techniques are from [How76]. Monitors are extensively used in concurrent programming. [BH77] and [BEW88] describe Pascal dialects that include monitor-based concurrent programming primitives. The books also include complete examples of systems written in these languages.

5.8   Exercises

1. Prove that the emulation of semaphores by monitors gives a blocked-queue semaphore.

2. Prove that the emulation of monitors by semaphores is no longer correct if blocked-set semaphores are used.

3. Program and prove the correctness of modifications to the solution to the problem of the readers and the writers which implement the following rules:

    *   If there are reading processes, a new reader may commence reading even if there are waiting writers.

---

[6] There is an implicit assumption that the data structure containing the processes trying to enter the monitor is also a FIFO queue.

- If there are waiting writers, they receive priority over all waiting readers.
- If there are waiting readers, no more than two writers will write before a process is allowed to read.

Chapter 6

The Problem of the Dining Philosophers

6.1 Introduction

The problem of the dining philosophers is a classic in the field of concurrent programming. While of little intrinsic interest, it offers an entertaining vehicle for comparing various formalisms for writing and proving concurrent programs. It is sufficiently simple to be tractable yet subtle enough to be challenging.

The problem is set in a secluded community of five philosophers. The philosophers engage in only two activities – *thinking* and *eating* (Figure 6.1).

```
task body Philosopher is
begin
  loop
    Think;
    Pre_Protocol;
    Eat;
    Post_Protocol;
  end loop;
end Philosopher;
```

Figure 6.1 Form of dining philosopher solution

Meals are taken communally at a table set with five plates and five forks (Figure 6.2). In the center of the table is a bowl of spaghetti that is endlessly replenished. Unfortunately, the spaghetti is hopelessly tangled and a philosopher needs two forks in order to eat.[1] Each philosopher may pick up the forks on his left and right, but only one at a time. The problem is to design pre- and post-protocols to ensure that a philosophers only eats if he has two forks. The solution should also satisfy the usual correctness properties that we described in the chapter on mutual exclusion. The set of correctness properties are:

---

[1] It is part of the folklore of computer science to point out that the story would be more believable if the bowl contained rice and the utensils were chopsticks.

1. A philosopher eats only if he has two forks.
2. No two philosophers may hold the same fork simultaneously.
3. No deadlock.
4. No individual starvation (pun intended).
5. Efficient behavior under absence of contention.

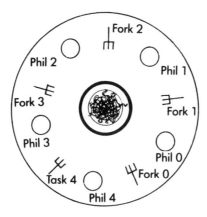

Figure 6.2 The dining table

6.2 Solutions using Semaphores

A first attempted solution is shown in Figure 6.3. We assume that each philosopher is initialized with its index *I*. Each fork is modeled as a semaphore. A philosopher must complete a `Wait` on both his left- and right-hand forks before eating.

```
Fork: array(0..4) of Semaphore := (others => 1);

task body Philosopher is
begin
  loop
    Think;
    Wait(Fork(I));
    Wait(Fork((I+1) mod 5));
    Eat;
    Signal(Fork(I));
    Signal(Fork((I+1) mod 5));
  end loop;
end Philosopher;
```

Figure 6.3 First attempt

Theorem 6.2.1 *No fork is ever held by two philosophers.*

Proof: The statement `Eat` is a critical section for each fork. If $\#Pi$ is the number of philosophers holding fork i then we have:

$$Fork(I) + \#Pi = 1$$

Together with the invariant that a semaphore is non-negative, we can conclude that $\#Pi \leq 1$. $\square$

Unfortunately, this solution deadlocks under an interleaving that has all philosophers pick up their left forks (i.e. execute `Wait(Fork(I))`) one after another before any of them tries to pick up a right fork. Now they are all waiting on their right forks, but no process will ever signal.

One way of ensuring liveness in a solution to the dining philosophers problem is to limit the number of philosophers entering the dining room to four (Figure 6.4).

```
Room: Semaphore := 4;
Fork: array(0..4) of Semaphore := (others => 1);

task body Philosopher is
begin
  loop
    Think;
    Wait(Room);
    Wait(Fork(I));
    Wait(Fork((I+1) mod 5));
    Eat;
    Signal(Fork(I));
    Signal(Fork((I+1) mod 5));
    Signal(Room);
  end loop;
end Philosopher;
```

Figure 6.4 Limit the number of philosophers

The addition of the `Room` semaphore obviously does not affect the correctness of the safety properties we showed in the last example.

Theorem 6.2.2 *Individual starvation cannot occur.*

Proof: We must assume that the `Room` semaphore is a blocked-queue semaphore so that any philosopher waiting to enter the room will eventually do so. The `Fork` semaphores need only be blocked-set semaphores since only two philosophers use each one.

Suppose philosopher i is starved. Then he is blocked forever on a semaphore. There are three cases depending on whether he is blocked on `Room`, `Fork(i)` or

Fork(i+1).[2]

Case 1: By the assumption that the semaphore is FIFO, i is blocked on Room only if its value is 0 indefinitely. By the semaphore invariant, this can happen only if the other four philosophers are blocked on forks, because if one of them should raise two forks and eat it will eventually finish eating, put down the forks and signal Room. Thus this case follows from the other two. Note that eating is considered to be a critical section which will eventually terminate.

Case 2: i is blocked on his left fork. Then philosopher $i - 1$ holds Fork(i) as his right fork. That is, philosopher $i - 1$ has successfully executed his last Wait statement and is either eating or signaling, both of eventually terminate releasing i.

Case 3: i is blocked on his right fork. This means that philosopher $i + 1$ has successfully taken his left fork (Fork(i+1)) and never released it. Since neither eating nor signaling can block, $i + 1$ must be suspended forever on his right fork. By induction, it follows that if i is blocked on his right fork, then so must all philosophers: $i + j, 0 \le j \le 4$. However, by the semaphore invariant on Room, for some $1 \le j \le 4$, philosopher $i + j$ is not in the room and thus obviously not blocked on a fork semaphore. □

Theorem 6.2.3 *Deadlock cannot occur.*

Proof: Immediate. □

Another solution that is free from starvation is the asymmetric solution (Figure 6.5) which has the first four philosophers execute the original solution, but the fifth philosopher waits first for the right fork and then for the left fork. Again it is obvious that the correctness properties on eating are satisfied. There cannot be deadlock or starvation. The proofs are similar to the previous one and are left as an exercise.

```
task body Philosopher is
begin
    Think;
    Wait(Fork(0));
    Wait(Fork(4));
    Eat;
    Signal(Fork(4));
    Signal(Fork(0));
  end loop;
end Philosopher;
```

Figure 6.5 Asymmetric solution to dining philosophers

---

[2] The computation of the index modulo 5 will not be explicitly noted in the proof.

6.3   Monitor Solutions to the Dining Philosophers

The difficulty with finding a semaphore solution to the problem of the dining philosophers is caused by the fact that executing a Wait on a semaphore is irrevocable. There is no way to test the value of two fork semaphores simultaneously. Using the monitor primitive, we can find an elegant solution by having a philosopher wait until both forks are free. Figure 6.6 is a monitor controlling the forks. Philosophers call the monitor as shown in Figure 6.7 to request forks. The process will leave the monitor only if it has two forks.

```
monitor Fork_Monitor
  Fork: array(0..4) of Integer range 0..2:=(others=>2);
  OK_to_Eat: array(0..4) of Condition;

procedure Take_Fork(I: Integer) is
begin
  if Fork(I) /= 2 then Wait(OK_to_Eat(I)); end if;
  Fork((I+1) mod 5) := Fork((I+1) mod 5)-1;
  Fork((I-1) mod 5) := Fork((I-1) mod 5)-1;
end Take_Fork;

procedure Release_Fork(I: Integer) is
begin
  Fork((I+1) mod 5) := Fork((I+1) mod 5)+1;
  Fork((I-1) mod 5) := Fork((I-1) mod 5)+1;
  if Fork((I+1) mod 5)=2 then
    Signal(OK_to_Eat((I+1) mod 5));
  end if;
  if Fork((I-1) mod 5)=2 then
    Signal(OK_to_Eat((I-1) mod 5));
  end if;
end Release_Fork;
end Fork_Monitor;
```

Figure 6.6 Monitor for dining philosophers

The monitor maintains an array Fork which counts the number of free forks available to each philosopher. The Take_Fork procedure waits on its own condition variable until two forks are available. Before leaving the monitor with these two forks, it decrements the number of free forks available to its neighbors. After eating, a philosopher calls Release_Fork. In addition to updating the available fork array, the procedure checks if freeing the forks makes it possible to signal a neighbor.

Theorem 6.3.1 *A philosopher eats only if he has two forks.*

Proof: It is an invariant that $Eating(I) \supset Fork(I) = 2$. Remember that a monitor invariant need only be true outside the monitor procedures. Then use

```
task body Philosopher is
begin
  loop
    Think;
    Take_Fork(I);
    Eat;
    Release_Fork(I);
  end loop;
end Philosopher;
```

Figure 6.7 Philosopher processes calling the monitor

the program code and the immediate resumption requirement. The details are left as an exercise. □

Theorem 6.3.2 *The solution does not deadlock.*

Proof: Let *eating* be the number of philosophers who have successfully completed Take_Fork to commence eating. Then the following two formulas can be proved invariant by the techniques used in the chapter on monitors:

$$Non\_Empty(OK\_to\_Eat(i)) \supset Fork(i) < 2 \qquad (6.1)$$

$$\sum_{i=0}^{4} Fork(i) = 10 - 2 * Eating \qquad (6.2)$$

Deadlock implies *Eating* = 0 and all philosophers are enqueued on OK_to_Eat. If no philosophers are eating, from (6.2) we conclude $\sum Fork(i) = 10$. If they are all enqueued waiting to eat, from (6.1) we conclude $\sum Fork(i) \leq 5$ which gives a contradiction in the value of *Fork*. □

However, this solution can cause starvation if two philosophers conspire to starve their mutual neighbor (Figure 6.8). Philosophers 1 and 3 both need a fork belonging to philosopher 2. If 1 finishes eating and puts fork 2 down, 2 cannot

Action	Fork(0)	Fork(1)	Fork(2)	Fork(3)	Fork(4)
(Initially)	2	2	2	2	2
Take_Fork(1)	1	2	1	2	2
Take_Fork(3)	1	2	0	2	1
Take_Fork(2) and					
Wait(OK_to_Eat(2))	1	2	0	2	1
Release_Fork(1)	2	2	1	2	1
Take_Fork(1)	1	2	0	2	1
Release_Fork(3)	1	2	1	2	2
Take_Fork(3)	1	2	0	2	1

Figure 6.8 Starvation of philosopher 2

start until 3 also finishes. If 1 tries to eat again before 3 has finished, he will find fork 2 still available and commence eating. Now philosopher 3 does the same thing and this interleaving can be continued indefinitely.

6.4   Further Reading

The dining philosophers problem has become a classic example ever since it was introduced by Dijkstra [Dij71].

Perfectly symmetrical solutions to problems in concurrent programming are impossible because if every process executes exactly the same program, they can never 'break ties'. All our algorithms contain asymmetries in the form of process identifiers or a kernel maintaining a queue. An interesting paper by Chandy and Misra [CM84] describes a starvation-free algorithm where precedence among the processes is indicated by a directed acyclic graph (see also [CM88]). The sink node with no outgoing edges has the highest priority. When that process has eaten it changes the graph to increase the precedence of other processes. After the modifications the graph is still acyclic. Though explicit process identifiers are no longer needed, the acyclic graph implicitly decides relative precedence.

6.5   Exercises

1. Prove the correctness of the asymmetric solution.

2. Investigate the dining philosophers problem for 2, 3 and 4 philosophers.

3. Program a solution that suffers from livelock. (*Hint:* A philosopher picks up his left fork and then checks if his right fork is free. If not he puts down his left fork and tries again.)

PART II

Distributed Programming

Chapter 7

Distributed Programming Models

7.1 Introduction

The concurrent programming abstractions of Part I are based on mutual exclusion on the access to an individual memory location or a system routine. Part II raises the level of abstraction to processes which *communicate* by sending *messages* to each other. Sending a message is a higher level action that can be easily implemented on physically distributed processors, hence the name given to this field: *distributed programming* or *distributed processing*.

As before, we will be dealing with an abstraction and not with the underlying implementation. In a physically distributed system, messages are exchanged along *communications channels* using *protocols* that define the format of a message as well as procedures for error detection and correction. The construction of such computer networks is beyond the scope of this book. Instead, our primitive notion will be that of sending and receiving a message. Unless otherwise indicated, we assume that a message arrives correctly – any error correction is done by the underlying protocol. Again, absolute time will not be used and messages may be delayed arbitrarily.

The high-level abstractions of distributed programming models are also used on single-processor computers, so the phrase 'send a message' need not imply the existence of a computer network. It can be implemented by calling a routine in an underlying operating system.

When designing primitives for distributed programming, there are a wide variety of decisions that must be made. The rest of this introductory chapter sets out the various options. The next three chapters describe languages – Ada, occam and Linda – whose designs are radically different on these points. Then we present some classical algorithms that are based on distributed programming models.

7.2 Synchronous or Asynchronous Communication

The common-memory models are based on regulating contention for a resource like a memory location or a monitor procedure. In the absence of contention, a single process need not be delayed. Communication, however, requires two processes – one to send a message and one to receive it. When a process sends a message, we must decide if the receiver must co-operate, that is if the receiver must be ready to receive the message when it is sent, or if the process can send one or more messages regardless of the state of the receiver.

In *synchronous communication* the exchange of a message is an atomic action requiring the participation of both the sending process – the *sender* – and the receiving process – the *receiver*. If the sender is ready to send but the receiver is not ready to receive, the sender is blocked and similarly, if the receiver is the first process ready to communicate, it blocks. The act of communication synchronizes the execution sequences of the two processes. The term *rendezvous* is often used to evoke an image of two processes that have to get to a designated point. The first process to arrive must wait for the second.

Alternatively, the sender is allowed to send a message and continue without blocking. The communication is called *asynchronous* because there is no time connection between the execution sequences of the two processes. The receiver could be executing any instructions when a message is sent and then, at a later time, check the communications channel for messages.

The important difference between the two schemes is the need for buffering messages. In asynchronous communication, the sender may send many messages without the receiver removing them from the channel. Thus the channel must be prepared to buffer a potentially unlimited number of messages. If the number of messages in the channel is limited, eventually the sender will be blocked. In synchronous communication, only one message exists at any one time on the channel so no buffering is needed.

The difference is analogous to that between the telephone system and the postal system. A telephone call synchronizes the activities of the caller and the person who answers. Difficulties with synchronization cause busy signals, unanswered calls, etc. On the other hand, any number of letters may be dropped in a mail box at any time and the receiver may choose to check the incoming mail at any time. There is no synchronization.

Unbuffered synchronous communication is the lower-level concept and hence more efficient. It is the primitive of choice in the models of occam and Ada. If buffers are needed, they must be explicitly programmed on top of the synchronous system, just as answering machines are built to allow a caller to buffer a message with the receiver rather than block.

The problem with an asynchronous system is that we have to specify the buffering system at the time the distributed *primitives* are being designed rather than leaving it to the individual programmer. The language Linda which is based on asynchronous communication offers unparalleled expressibility and convenience at increased implementation cost.

7.3 Process Identification

A telephone company can install a line that directly connects two telephones. Such a dedicated line is usually of higher quality and speed than one that is temporarily set up by the ordinary switching system. However, it is not flexible since it takes time to install and is very expensive.

Switching equipment allows any telephone to call any other. To call, the originator of the call must know the identification — the telephone number — of the destination, but the receiver cannot know the identification of the caller unless the caller explicitly chooses to pass on this information. Another way of saying this is that the caller may be anonymous, but not the receiver.

A more flexible means of communication is a bulletin board. Here both parties may choose to remain anonymous: an unsigned message may be posted and anyone is able to read or remove the message.

All these forms of naming are used in distributed models:

occam Dedicated channels connecting pairs of processes.

Ada A process calls another process by name without divulging its own identity.

Linda Broadcast messages (that need not be signed with a process identifier).

Dedicated channels are the most efficient since every message can be delivered with no overhead cost of deciphering addresses. However, any modification of the system entails changing the source code of the program.

The Ada asymmetric system is best suited to writing *server* processes, like a disk driver. Any process that knows the name of the server can request and receive the service that the process implements. The server need not be concerned with the identity of the requesters. Adding additional processes which need the same service to the system can thus be done without modification of source code.

Without process identifiers, the flexibility of the system is greatly improved since it is possible to add, remove or modify processes dynamically. For example, suppose that a system that used one type of disk drive was upgraded to use two different types. The new driver would have its own process name and we would have to change all requesting processes or at least write an additional process to route the requests. In Linda, one can simply add the needed driver and it will remove and process requests with no other change to the system.

7.4 Data Flow

A single act of communication can have data flowing in one direction or two. A telegram or letter causes data to flow in one direction only. A reply requires a separate act of communication. A telephone call allows two-way communication. While it is true that one party must call the other party by number, once the connection is made data can flow both ways.

Asynchronous systems (Linda) use one-way data flow since the sender can send the message and then continue. If the receiver is not ready, obviously it cannot return data to the sender and a separate message is needed.

In synchronous systems, a channel is set up between two processes and a decision must be made whether to implement one-way (occam) or two-way data flow (Ada). As usual, there is a tradeoff between expressibility and efficiency, though care is needed when comparing the two designs for efficiency. It is true that sending a single message on a one-way channel is extremely efficient, because all that is needed is an acknowledgement of correct transmission and the sender need not be blocked while the receiver processes the message and decides if a reply is needed. However, if *most* messages do in fact need a reply, it may be more efficient to block the sender rather than release it and later go through the overhead of a new message for the reply.

7.5   Process Creation

Do all processes in a concurrent program exist when the program commences execution, or can processes be created dynamically? This question is not restricted to distributed systems, but it is convenient to discuss here since the three formalisms make different choices. As usual, a static definition of the set of processes (occam) is most efficient since the implementation can be done in terms of directly accessible compiled routines, memory locations, or channel numbers. There are several reasons that one would want the ability to create processes during execution.

Flexibility A system can be designed and programmed without knowing how many processes will be needed. During initialization, or upon request, processes can be allocated. For example, an operating system may allocate a process to each connected terminal. As the number of terminals changes, so can the number of allocated processes. On a static system, there would be a built-in limit to the number of connected terminals.

Dynamic use of resources A system may need different sets of resources at different times. With dynamic allocation, the number of processes for each resource can be matched with the requirements. This both saves the memory needed for process descriptors and also improves efficiency since implementations of concurrency may have algorithms that depend on the number of processes.

Load balancing In a multi-processor system, one possible design is to allocate a processor to each separate function. If one function temporarily requires increased computational power, there is little that can be done. However, if dynamic process creation is available, additional processes can be created to perform the overloaded function and assigned to underutilized processors. When the load on this function is reduced, the extra processes can be terminated and the processors allocated to other tasks.

Static process creation is most applicable in embedded systems like aircraft control systems or medical monitoring systems where the configuration of the system is fixed and predictability of performance is more important than flexibility. Since the configuration of the computer is also fixed, load balancing is not important. On a large transaction processing system, like an airline reservation system, dynamic process creation is important. The computing requirements change during the day and the system must not be halted during configuration changes needed to maintain the system or to keep it running during partial equipment failures.

7.6 Further Reading

A collection of articles that surveys the field of distributed programming can be found in [CDJ84]. Case studies of real systems can help motivate the study of distributed programming. Two that are relevant are [GS84] which describes an airline reservations system and [SG84] which describes the avionics system of a spacecraft.

Chapter 8

Ada

8.1 Introduction

Ada is a comprehensive programming language developed for the US Department of Defense as the standard language for critical software systems. Ada uses strong typing for reliability and a construct called *packages* for decomposition of large systems into modules. Our interest is in a third aspect of the language: the provision of built-in primitives for concurrent programming. Earlier languages supported only sequential programming; concurrent programming was done by directly calling the underlying operating system or by creating an operating system directly on the computer hardware. This made it practically impossible to port programs from one system to another. By including a model of concurrent programming, called *tasking* in the standard language, Ada makes this possible.

This chapter discusses Ada tasking in some detail. The model is very powerful and we can naturally express most concurrent algorithms in the language. We will also examine some of the shortcomings of Ada tasking. In the next two chapters, we will sketch the main ideas of two other concurrent programming models which took radically different decisions in the conflict between expressibility and efficiency.

Because Ada is an excellent and highly available language, it has been chosen as the unifying notation in this book. However, this is not a textbook on the language and simplifications or omissions may exist where a complete description would have caused too far a digression from our main subject. Several good texts on Ada are listed in the references for those who will actually use the language.

8.2 Rendezvous

Communication in Ada is synchronous (and unbuffered). Two tasks[1] must meet in a *rendezvous* in order to communicate. The name is chosen to invoke the image of two people who choose a place to meet (Figure 8.1(a)). The first one to arrive must wait for the arrival of the second.

---

[1] To conform with Ada terminology, processes will be called tasks in this chapter.

In this image, the two people are symmetric and the rendezvous is neutral. In Ada, however, the location of the rendezvous belongs to one of the tasks, called the *accepting* task. The other task, the *calling* task, must know the identity of the accepting task and the name of the location of the rendezvous (Figure 8.1(b)), called the *entry*. The accepting task, however, does not know the identity of the calling task. It is important to emphasize that both tasks are executing concurrently and they only synchronize at the rendezvous.

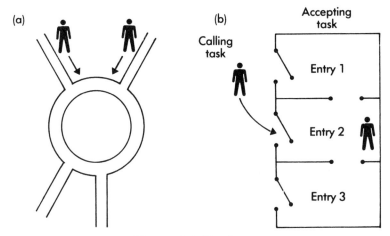

Figure 8.1 Rendezvous

The advantage of the asymmetric model is that *servers* can be naturally programmed. For example, the accepting task could be a printer server which will be willing to accept requests to print from any other task in the system. If a symmetric naming system were used, the programming of the server task would have to be changed every time a new task is added.

Let us turn to the definition of the rendezvous in Ada. A task is divided into two sections, the *specification* and the *body*. The specification may only contain declarations of *entries*.[2] Syntactically, an entry is exactly like a procedure declaration. This is done on purpose to allow substitution of a concurrent entry for a sequential procedure without otherwise changing a program.

```
task Buffer is
   entry Append(I: in  Integer);
   entry Take  (I: out Integer);
end Buffer;
```

Once a task specification has been declared and made visible to other tasks, they may call the entry using dotted notation – the task name followed by the entry name and appropriate parameters:

```
Buffer.Append(I);
```

---

[2] Until now, we have not used entries so we have omitted the task specification. However, every task must have a specification, even if it is null.

If `Append` were a procedure, control would be transferred immediately to the procedure body. An entry call must rendezvous with an `accept` statement in the task owning the entry:

```
task body Buffer is
begin
   ...
   accept Append(I: in Integer) do
      ... statements in the accept body
   end Append;
   ...
end Buffer;
```

Remember, the accepting task is an ordinary sequential process, executing its instructions. Like other instructions, the `accept` statement is executed in sequence when the instruction pointer reaches it, except that its definition requires synchronization with a calling task. In the assumed interleaving of execution sequences, either the calling task reaches the entry call before the accepting task reaches an accept statement for this entry, or conversely. Whichever task is first will suspend until the other reaches its matching statement. At that point, the rendezvous commences. The semantics of a rendezvous are as follows:

1. The calling task passes its `in` parameters to the accepting task and is blocked pending completion of the rendezvous.

2. The accepting task executes the statements in the accept *body* (the statements following the `do` up to the matching `end`).

3. The `out` parameters are passed back to the calling task.

4. The rendezvous is now complete and both tasks are no longer suspended.

Note that the completion of the rendezvous does not necessarily cause a task to commence execution. The decision of which task will execute is left to the underlying scheduler. The completion of a rendezvous completes the execution of the `accept` statement. If the task wishes to engage in an additional rendezvous, it must execute another `accept` statement. A typical non-terminating task, like a server, will have an accept statement in a loop so that it can engage in multiple rendezvous.

Figure 8.2 demonstrates the `accept` statement on a program that maintains a degenerate bounded buffer. Producer tasks will call the `Append` entry and consumer tasks will call the `Take` entry. The `accept` statements have been placed in a loop so that after each pair of rendezvous (between a producer and the buffer and then between a consumer and the buffer) the buffer task will re-issue the `accept Append` statement.

Comparing this solution with the monitor solution, we find that the buffer has become a separate task rather than just a passive set of data and procedures. However, even though there is the overhead of an additional task, on a multi-processor implementation the Ada solution could be more efficient since not all of the processing has to be done within the mutual exclusion of the rendezvous. In this case, updating the indices and the counter need not be done in the rendezvous since they are local variables. This structure is typical of Ada algorithms since

```
task body buffer is
  B: array(0..N-1) of Integer;
  In_Ptr, Out_Ptr: Integer := 0;
  Count: Integer := 0;

begin
  loop
    accept Append(I: in Integer) do
      B(In_Ptr) := I;
    end Append;
    Count := Count + 1;
    In_Ptr := (In_Ptr + 1) mod N;
    accept Take(I: out Integer) do
      I := B(Out_Ptr);
    end Take;
    Count := Count - 1;
    Out_Ptr := (Out_Ptr + 1) mod N;
  end loop;
end Buffer;
```

Figure 8.2 Degenerate bounded buffer

synchronization is defined directly between tasks and not through the agency of an operating system.

The entries belong to the task which declares them and only it can execute **accept** statements for them. While the accepting task can have many **accept** statements (even for the same entry), it can obviously only execute one statement at a time. However, several tasks can call the same entry in another task. For example, several producers could call **Buffer.Append** concurrently. Tasks calling the same entry are enqueued in order of arrival on the entry. Each **accept** statement engages in a rendezvous with the first task in its entry queue. Completion of the **accept** body completes the rendezvous; the accepting task does *not* continue to engage in rendezvous with the tasks in the entry queue. Instead, it must execute another **accept** for this entry (i.e. another occurrence of an **accept** statement, which may be the same statement encountered after looping).

To summarize, the Ada rendezvous is a primitive with the following characteristics:

- Synchronous, unbuffered communication.
- Asymmetric identification – the sender knows the identity of the receiver, but not conversely.
- Two-way data flow during a single rendezvous.

Global variables that are shared among several tasks are also allowed in Ada but we refer the reader to an Ada textbook for a description of this feature. They have been used to program the examples in Chapter 3 in Ada.

8.3   The Select Statement

The solution given in Figure 8.2 is degenerate because it contains no provision
for refusing a rendezvous with a full or empty buffer. Also, it prescribes a strict
alternation between producing and consuming which is not the definition of a
buffer. This section presents the `select` statement which allows a task to select
an entry call to execute from among several alternatives and also to conditionally
accept an entry call. Before describing the `select` statement in full generality,
let us look at a correct solution for the bounded buffer (Figure 8.3).

```
task body Buffer is
  B: array(0..N-1) of Integer;
  In_Ptr, Out_Ptr: Integer := 0;
  Count: Integer := 0;

begin
  loop
    select
      when Count < N =>
        accept Append(I: in Integer) do
          B(In_Ptr) := I;
        end Append;
      Count := Count + 1;
      In_Ptr := (In_Ptr + 1) mod N;
    or
      when Count > 0 =>
        accept Take(I: out Integer) do
          I := B(Out_Ptr);
        end Take;
      Count := Count - 1;
      Out_Ptr := (Out_Ptr + 1) mod N;
    end select;
  end loop;
end Buffer;
```

Figure 8.3 Bounded buffer

The `select` statement enables the buffer to choose non-deterministically between two *guarded* alternatives. The guards are boolean expressions prefixed to
each `accept` statement. If the expression evaluates to true, the alternative is
called an *open* alternative and a rendezvous with the `accept` statement is permitted. If the expression evaluates to false the alternative is said to be *closed* and
rendezvous is not permitted.

In the example, if the buffer is empty $Count = 0$, the `select` statement is reduced to an ordinary `accept` statement on the remaining open alternative `Append`.
If the buffer is full $Count = N$, there will also be only one open alternative. It
is important to note that at least one alternative must always be open since it is

impossible that $Count = 0$ and $Count = N$ simultaneously.[3]

If $0 < Count < N$, both alternatives are open. If there are no tasks waiting in the entry queues, the accepting task will wait for the first task that calls an entry. Unlike the algorithm in the previous section which required a call from the consumer after every call from the producer, the use of the **select** statement enables the buffer to rendezvous with whichever task calls it first.

If there are calling tasks waiting in only one of the entry queues, a rendezvous will take place with the first task in that queue. However, if there are calling tasks waiting in both entry queues, the accepting task non-deterministically chooses to rendezvous with the first task in one of the two queues. By this is meant that the implementation is free to choose between the open alternatives according to any (reasonable) algorithm. Non-deterministic does not mean random, which implies that it impossible to predict which choice will be taken. An implementation that always chooses the first open alternative is a correct implementation. The meaning of non-determinism for the programmer is that the correctness of the program cannot depend on the actual algorithm chosen. In the case of the bounded buffer, this is true. If one alternative were consistently favored, eventually the buffer would fill up (or become empty), the favored alternative would be closed by its guard and the other alternative would have to be chosen.

We now give the full definition of the **select** statement. Syntactically, a **select** statement consists of an arbitrary number of guarded **accept** statements separated by the reserved word **or**. A guard may be omitted, in which case it is assumed to be **when True =>**. Following each **accept** statement, a sequence of statements may be written. Finally, the last alternative of the **select** may be one of:

- **else** followed by a sequence of statements.
- **delay** T followed by a sequence of statements. T is a real-valued expression.
- **terminate**.

These special alternatives are mutually exclusive, that is, only one of them can appear.

The semantics of the **select** statement are as follows:

1. The guards are evaluated. The set of alternatives whose guards evaluate to true is called the set of open alternatives. It is a fatal error if the set of open alternatives is empty (unless there is an **else** alternative).

2. If there are calling tasks waiting on entry queues for open alternatives, a rendezvous is commenced with the first task on one of those queues.

3. If all queues for open alternatives are empty, the accepting task is suspended. As soon as some task calls an entry in the set of open alternatives, the rendezvous is commenced with this calling task. Note that the set of open alternatives does not change, because the guards are not re-evaluated during the execution of the **select** statement.

4. The rendezvous is conducted as follows:

---

[3] As usual assuming the size of the buffer is greater than zero.

- The in parameters are passed from the calling task to the accepting task.
- The calling task is suspended.
- The accepting task executes the statements in the accept body.
- The out parameters are passed from the accepting task back to the calling task.
- The calling task is released from suspension.

5. Upon completion of the rendezvous, the accepting task executes the statements following the accept body.

6. select with else alternative. If there are no open alternatives, or if there are open alternatives but no calling task is in one of their entry queues, the sequence of statements in the else alternative is executed.

7. select with delay alternative. If there are no calling tasks in the entry queues of the open alternatives, the accepting task will wait as described above, but only for the amount of time given in the delay clause. When this time has expired, the sequence of statements in the delay alternative is executed. It is important to emphasize that the accepting task need not be awakened *exactly* when the delay has expired, only that if the entry queues are still empty after the delay has expired, the task can be rescheduled and will execute the statements in the delay alternative.

8. select with terminate alternative. A complete explanation of this alternative is beyond the scope of this book. Roughly, if this select statement is suspended and all tasks which could possibly call its entries have completed execution or are also waiting on select statements with terminate alternatives, then this entire set of tasks is terminated.

As can be seen, the select statement is a powerful yet elementary concurrent programming primitive. It is doing a relatively efficient low-level operation: checking for calls and choosing among them, but the various options make it possible to express many algorithms in a natural way.

8.4   Programming with the Rendezvous

The expressive power of the rendezvous is not apparent from the description of its semantics. In this section, we will present several paradigms that demonstrate the generality of the rendezvous.

A simple rendezvous implements a *remote procedure call*. The calling task calls a 'procedure' that is not present within itself, but instead belongs to another independent task. The select is a generalization of the remote procedure call.

The delay alternative implements a *timeout*: a limit on the amount of time one is willing to wait. It can be used in control systems that require the program to sense the absence of a response and not just to interpret a response (Figure 8.4).

The else alternative is equivalent to a delay of zero. This implements a form of *polling*: check if there is a message that needs to be processed, otherwise continue with the normal processing. This is not the same as doing background

```
task body T is
begin
  loop
    select
      accept Sensor_1 do ... ;
    or
      accept Sensor_2 do ...;
    or
      . . .
    or
      delay 0.1;  -- 100 milliseconds
      Raise_Alarm;
    end select;
  end loop;
end T;
```

Figure 8.4 Timeout

processing which requires an extra task which can work while the accepting task waits for a response (Figure 8.5). The statements in the **else** alternative are ordinary sequential statements that are part of the accepting task. The **select** will not be re-issued until those statements are completed and a new cycle of the loop begins.

```
task body Foreground is
begin
  loop
    select
      accept A1 ... ;
    or
      accept A2 ... ;
    or
      . . .
    end select;
  end loop;
end Foreground;

task body Background is
begin
  loop
    . . .
  end loop;
end Background;
```

Figure 8.5 Background processing

The **accept** bodies may be empty. Null **accept** bodies are used for synchronization of tasks. The classic example is the emulation of binary semaphores by

```
task body Semaphore is
begin
  loop
    accept Wait;
    accept Signal;
  end loop;
end Semaphore;
```

Figure 8.6 Emulation of semaphores in Ada

an Ada task given in Figure 8.6.[4] Note again that an 'operating system' service
has become an independent task.

The true power of the rendezvous becomes apparent when we realize that
the statements within a rendezvous are not restricted to ordinary sequential programming statements, but may include tasking statements such as entry calls,
or accept statements. For example, it is possible to synchronize three tasks together by having one of them issue nested accept statements for the other two
(Figure 8.7). Task T2 will remain suspended until the rendezvous with T3 has
occurred. If T3 calls T1 first, it will wait in the entry queue until T2 arrives, which
is what we want anyway. If the accept statements were not nested, T2 could be
rescheduled before T3 calls its entry.

```
task body T1 is
begin
  ...
  accept Synch_2 do   -- T2 calls this entry
    accept Synch_3;   -- T3 calls this entry
  end Synch_2;
  ...
end T1;
```

Figure 8.7 Three-way rendezvous

We have emphasized the distinction between the text of an accept or select
statement and the execution of such a statement, which like any other statement
has a well-defined semantics, and executes to completion. Our algorithms have
used loops to re-issue the statements. However, there is nothing to prevent there
being several accept statements for the same entry. In Figure 8.8 we show an
outline of a solution to the problem of the readers and the writers which uses
additional accept statements to ensure that the data are initialized by a write
before any reads are permitted. In Figure 8.9, there are separate accept statements for processing even and odd calls. The important point to remember is that
the queues are associated with the *entries* and not with the accept statements.

---

[4] This is a degenerate implementation of a binary semaphore initialized to 1 that can be used
to solve the mutual exclusion problem. A better implementation of semaphores in Ada can be
found in Appendix B.

```
task body Readers_and_Writers is
begin
  accept Start_Write;
  accept End_Write;
  loop
    select
      accept Start_Read ... ;
    or
      accept End_Read ...;
    or
      accept Start_Write ... ;
    or
      accept End_Write ... ;
    end select;
  end loop;
end Readers_and_Writers;
```

Figure 8.8 Initializing rendezvous

```
task body Even_Odd is
begin
  loop
    accept E(...) do
      -- process odd calls
    end E;
    accept E(...) do
      -- process even calls
    end E;
  end loop;
end Even_Odd;
```

Figure 8.9 Even odd rendezvous

8.5   Select in the Calling Task

Just as the accepting task can use **else** and **delay** alternatives to avoid being suspended forever waiting for a rendezvous, a similar facility is available to the calling task. There is an essential difference between the calling task and the accepting task, because the calling task can only suspend waiting for one entry. There are no multi-entry calls.

Figure 8.10 shows an example of timeout in the calling task. If a call is not accepted within the time interval specified, the attempt is abandoned and the statements following the **delay** are executed. This does not mean that the calling task will be suspended for the time interval since the rendezvous itself could take arbitrarily long and even upon completion of the rendezvous the calling task might not be immediately scheduled.

Figure 8.11 shows the use of the **else** clause to successively poll several servers. The calling task engages in a rendezvous only if a server is immediately available. Otherwise, the attempt is abandoned and the task continues to the next **select**

statement. This version will engage in a rendezvous with all of the servers that
are waiting. Figure 8.12 shows how to rendezvous with exactly one server.

```
task body T is
begin
  loop
    select
      Sensor.Sample(...);
    or
      delay 1.0; -- seconds
      Notify_Operator;
    end select;
  end loop;
end T;
```

Figure 8.10 Timeout of the calling task

```
task body T is
begin
  loop
    select
      Server_1.E(...);
    else
      null;
    end select;
    select
      Server_2.E(...);
    else
      null;
    end select;
    ...
  end loop;
end T;
```

Figure 8.11 Polling one or more servers

8.6   Dynamic Task Creation

The Ada tasks we have seen are static. The data structures needed to support
the task (instruction pointer, memory allocation, task control block) are created
when the program is initially loaded[5] and the task remains in existence until the
end of the program.

---

[5] The situation in Ada is more complicated than described here. The creation process is called
elaboration and depends on the modular structure of the program. A description of elaboration
is beyond the scope of this book.

```
task body T is
begin
  loop
    select
      Server_1.E(...);
    else
      select
        Server_2.E(...);
      else
        ...
      end select;
    end select;
  end loop;
end T;
```

Figure 8.12 Polling at most one server

It is also possible to declare a task *type* and then create a data structure of tasks using this template, just as if the task type were an ordinary record type. Of course we cannot add or subtract task values – the only operations allowed are entry calls and passing the task as a parameter. Each variable declared with this task type causes a new task *object* to be created. These task objects execute the same code defined in the body associated with the task type, but they are allocated new variables.

In Figure 8.13, a task type Buffer_Type has been declared followed by an array of tasks Buffers. They each execute the same code, but the buffer array, pointers and counter are distinct for each object. Next a procedure has been declared that takes a task of this type as a parameter. The two executable statements in Figure 8.13 show a call to an entry point of an element of the task array and a call to the procedure. Note that the identity of the task called is computed at run-time.

Additional flexibility can be achieved by declaring pointers to task types. In Ada, once a pointer type (called an *access type*) has been declared, additional objects of the type can be allocated during *execution*. Using the usual techniques of data structures it is possible to maintain a list of tasks which can be created at run-time (Figure 8.14). A node is declared which contains a field of (task) type Buffer_Type and a pointer to the same node type. The procedure allocates a new node (*including* a new task) and links it after the node pointed to by the parameter.[6]

8.7 Priorities and Entry Families

A priority can be associated with an Ada task by inserting the following clause in the task specification:[7]

---

[6] The parameter is assumed non-null.

[7] A *pragma* is an instruction to the compiler. Ada compilers need not implement every pragma.

```
task type Buffer_Type is
  entry Append(I: in  Integer);
  entry Take  (I: out Integer);
end Buffer_Type;

Buffers: array(1..20) of Buffer_Type;

procedure P(Buff: in Buffer_Type) is
  I: Integer := ...;
begin
  Buff.Append(I);            -- call entry in parameter
end P;

Buffers(I+1).Append(E1);   -- direct call

P(Buffers(J));             -- task parameter
```

Figure 8.13 An array of buffer tasks

```
type Node;
type Buffer_Ptr is access Node;
type Node is
  record
    Buff: Buffer_Type;
    Next: Buffer_Ptr;
  end record;

procedure Allocate(Ptr: in out Buffer_Ptr) is
  Temp: Buffer_Ptr := Ptr.Next;
begin
  Ptr.Next := new Node;
  Ptr.Next.Next := Temp;
end Allocate;
```

Figure 8.14 A list of tasks

```
pragma Priority(N);
```

where N is an integer literal in a range defined by the implementation. The priority is static and may not be changed during execution of the program.

Priorities are only used to influence scheduling of the tasks. They do not participate in the choice of **select** alternatives and certainly do not change the FIFO requirement of the entry queues. A *synchronization point* is a point in the computation where a scheduling decision must be made, for example, at the conclusion of a rendezvous. At a synchronization point, if there are several tasks of the highest priority ready to execute, the scheduler must choose one of them as the next task to proceed. A rendezvous between two tasks of different priorities is executed at the higher of two priorities.

An implementation must use a *pre-emptive* scheduler – if the delay on a high-priority task expires, the scheduler must interrupt a lower priority task in its favor.

An implementation may employ *time-slicing* which uses a timer to suspend the computation at a pre-defined time interval. Then the scheduler is called to search for another task. In Chapter 16 we discuss a problem known as *priority inversion* that can occur in Ada because of the interaction between pre-emption and the rendezvous.

A server task that accepts calls according to priority can be programmed using a facility in Ada called *entry families*. This is similar to an array of entries in a single task. In Figure 8.15 we have defined three priority levels.[8] By

```
type Priorities is (Low, Medium, High);

task Server is
  entry Request(Priorities)(...);
end Server;

task body Server is
begin
  loop
    select
      accept Request(High)(...) ... ;
    or
      when Request(High)'Count = 0 =>
        accept Request(Medium)(...) ... ;
    or
      when Request(High)'Count = 0 and
           Request(Medium)'Count = 0 =>
        accept Request(Low)(...) ... ;
    end select;
  end loop;
end Server;

Server.Request(High)(...);  -- syntax of call
```

Figure 8.15 Entry families for priority

declaring a family member for each priority, guards can be used to close alternatives for lower priority calls when a higher priority call is waiting. The expression **Request(High)'Count** is called an *attribute*. Its value is the number of tasks waiting in an entry queue.

There is a potential problem in this program. Suppose a high priority task places a timeout on its call to the server using **select** with an **else** or **delay** alternative. If the timeout occurs *after* the evaluation of the guards, but *before* selecting an alternative, the server task could be blocked indefinitely waiting for another high priority caller.

This solution works for a small number of priorities. If the entry family is large, it is possible to poll them, but this does not seem like a satisfactory solution (Figure 8.16).

---

[8] These priorities are not connected with the scheduling priorities.

```
type Priorities is range 1..100;

for I in Priorities loop
  select
    accept Request(I)(...) ... ;
  else
    null;
  end select;
end loop;
```

Figure 8.16 Polling a large family

8.8   Further Reading

The definition of the Ada standard is [DOD83]. Ada textbooks contain more or less complete descriptions of the tasking facility, while [Bur85] is devoted entirely to the subject. His development of algorithms for resource allocation touches on all the fine points of Ada tasking.

Chapter 9

occam

9.1 Introduction

The concurrent programming model of occam is also based on the rendezvous
that is used in Ada. In fact, the models are so similar that it is easier to present
occam in terms of the differences between it and Ada than to present the language
from first principles. It should be emphasized that the similarity applies only to
the concurrent programming model and not to the other aspects of the languages
which are in fact rather different. In addition, the syntax of occam is unusual.
The ideas will be presented as modifications of Ada syntax, and a final section in
this chapter will give an overview of occam syntax.

9.2 Concurrent Programming in occam

In Ada, a rendezvous is conducted at an **accept** or **select** statement *belonging*
to a task. The calling task must know the name of the accepting task, the name
of the entry and the parameter *signature* (the number and types of the parameters). In occam, two processes communicate via *channels* which are declared
in a scope visible to both processes. Associated with each channel is a *protocol*
defining the signature of the data that can flow through the channel (Figure 9.1).
Communication is between output statements (similar to the Ada entry call) and
corresponding input statements (similar to the Ada **accept**).

An occam compiler checks that every channel is used to connect exactly *two*
processes, one of which performs output statements only and the other input
statements only. In addition, processes are statically declared and cannot be
allocated at run-time. Thus the complete topology of the processes and their
interconnections via channels is known before commencing execution.

occam is very strict about restricting interprocess communication to rendezvous. In particular, Load-Store to common memory does not exist. If a global
variable is assigned to in one process, it may not be accessed (load or store) by
any other process.

There is a statement (called **ALT**) comparable to the Ada **select** with guards
and **else** and **delay** alternatives. There is no **terminate** alternative – termination

```
type Protocol_1 is
  record
    I: Integer;
    C: Character;
  end record;

type Channel_1 is channel of Protocol_1;

Ch1, Ch2: Channel_1;

Output(Ch1)(23,'a');   -- In process P1
Input (Ch1)(I, C);     -- In process P2
```

Figure 9.1 occam channels

must be programmed explicitly. On the other hand, there are two useful features of this statement which are missing in Ada. One is prioritized choice of alternatives (Figure 9.2). If there are several open alternatives waiting for rendezvous, the first open alternative in textual order will be chosen. Remember that in Ada we

```
prioritized select
  accept E1 ... ;   -- First choice
or
  accept E2 ... ;   -- Second choice
or
  ..
end select;
```

Figure 9.2 Prioritized alternate

found the entry family feature limiting because each family member had to be programmed explicitly, or we had to poll each member in a **select** statement with an **else** alternative. In occam, it is possible to use a repetitive construct to wait on all members of a family simultaneously (Figure 9.3). The first call to any member of the family will be accepted.

```
type Priorities is range 0..100;

for I in Priorities select
  accept Request(I)(...) do
    ...
  end Request;
end select;
```

Figure 9.3 Repetitive alternate

9.3 Matrix Multiplication in occam

Except for the extra features of the alternative rendezvous, occam primitives are a subset of the Ada primitives and the examples of occam programming can easily be translated into Ada. In this section we will present a classic example of an occam program which demonstrates the flavor of the language. The example is matrix multiplication by an array of processes (Figure 9.4).

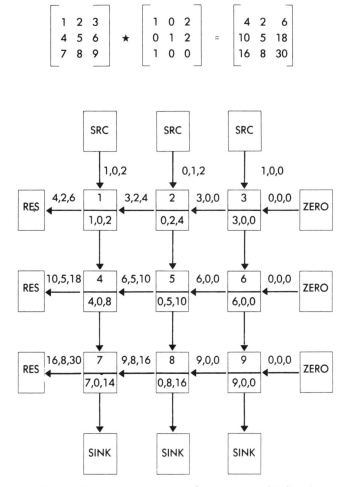

Figure 9.4 Processor array for matrix multiplication

To multiply a matrix X (or a sequence of matrices) by a fixed matrix A, we allocate a process for each element A_{ij}. The elements of X are fed in from the top and the partial sums are passed from right to left until they emerge from the

array of processes with the final result. At the right are a set of processes that
feed in zeros to initialize the sums and at the bottom are sink processes to absorb
the elements of X as they leave the bottom row. These are necessary so that all
processes associated with the matrix elements are identical and need not know if
they are at a particular edge of the array. Before proceeding further, the reader
is advised to work out the example in Figure 9.4 by hand to be sure that the
computation is understood.

```
task body Multiplier_Task is
  X, Sum, A: Integer;
  North, South, East, West: Channel;
begin
  accept Init(I: Integer; N, S, E, W: Channel) do
    A := I;
    North := N; South := S; East := E; West := W;
  end Init;
  loop
    accept Input(North)(I: in Integer) do
      X := I;
    end Input;
    Output(South)(X);
    accept Input(East) (I: in Integer) do
      Sum := I;
    end Input;
    Sum := Sum + A*X;
    Output(West) (Sum);
  end loop;
end Multiplier_Task;
```

Figure 9.5 Multiplier Tasks

Figure 9.5 shows the multiplier tasks. Each of the N by N tasks will be task
objects of this task type. The system is configured by calling the entry Init from
the main program to pass the array element **A** and the channel identification to
the task. Then the task enters a loop to perform the required multiplications and
data transfers:

1. Get a vector element from **North**.
2. Pass it to **South**.
3. Get a partial sum from **East**.
4. Perform the multiplication and update the partial sum.
5. Transfer the new result to **West**.

Figure 9.6 shows the code for the four types of task around the boundary
of the array of multiplier tasks (except that the initialization has been omitted).
The main program must declare all the channels (there are 24) and initialize the
processes with the correct channel numbers.

We certainly do not claim that this is the most efficient way of programming
matrix multiplication, even in occam. However, the example does demonstrate the
philosophy of occam programming: a large number of small concurrent processes,

communicating by fast channels rather than using synchronization of access to global variables.

```
task body Source_Task is
  Vec: Vector;
begin
  -- Get vector
  for N in Vector'Range loop
    Output(South)(Vec(N));
  end loop;
end Source_Task;

task body Sink_Task is
begin
  loop
    accept Input(North)(I: in Integer);
  end loop;
end Sink_Task;

task body Zero_Task is
begin
  loop
    Output(West)(0);
  end loop;
end Zero_Task;

task body Result_Task is
  Vec: Vector;
begin
  for N in Vector'Range loop
    accept Input(E)(I: in Integer) do
      Vec(N) := I;
    end Input;
  end loop;
  -- Print result
end Result_Task;
```

Figure 9.6 Boundary tasks

9.4   occam Syntax

It is worthwhile to touch on certain features of occam syntax, because one can see here the effect that syntax can have on programming style.

In occam, *every* statement – even a lowly assignment statement – is considered to be a process. It is up to the programmer to indicate *explicitly* whether statements will be combined in sequence or in parallel (Figure 9.7). Compare this with Ada which uses simple juxtaposition to indicate sequential execution, but requires a task specification and task body to indicate parallelism. Thus occam

```
SEQ
  statement_1
  statement_2
  statement_3

PAR
  statement_1
  statement_2
  statement_3
```

Figure 9.7 Sequential versus parallel execution

encourages concurrent programming by setting its syntax on an equal footing with sequential programming.

In Ada, entry call and accept use a notation that is designed to mimic procedures so that a service can be changed from a procedure to a task with minimal modification of the user programs. In occam, communication is denoted by a distinct notation: **channel ? variable** for input and **channel ! value** for output. Figure 9.8 shows the multiplier task in occam. Note the use of indentation rather than punctuation (';' in Ada) to show program structure.

```
WHILE TRUE
  SEQ
    north ? x
    south ! x
    east  ? sum
    sum := sum + a * x
    west  ! sum
```

Figure 9.8 Multiplier tasks in occam syntax

It is easy to modify this program to take advantage of additional parallelism in the algorithm (Figure 9.9). The transfer of the value to the south and the multiplication of the value and the matrix element can take place in parallel with waiting for the partial sum from the east. Similarly, the transfer of the result can take place in parallel with waiting for the next value from the north.

```
north ? x
  WHILE TRUE
    SEQ
      PAR
        south ! x
        east  ? sum
        temp := a * x
      PAR
        west  ! sum + temp
        north ? x
```

Figure 9.9 Multiplier tasks with parallelism

9.5 Further Reading

occam is based on the concurrent programming primitives called CSP [Hoa78]. CSP has been intensively studied in theoretical investigations of concurrency [Hoa85]. An introduction to occam is given in [PM87]. The reference manual is [In88]. Jones and Goldsmith [JG88] give complete programs in occam including the matrix multiplication example.

Chapter 10

Linda

10.1 Introduction

Linda is an experimental concurrent programming concept that is radically different from the concepts we have studied so far. However, unlike Ada or occam which are fully developed production-quality languages, Linda has been experimentally embedded in several languages. In the following overview, we will use Ada syntax.

Ada and occam are both based on the idea of synchronous communications channels between processes. At any point in time during the execution of a program in these languages, there is a well-defined set of process, connected in some topology and these processes can engage in synchronous rendezvous along the channels. There is *coupling* in both *time* and *space*.

Time The synchronous rendezvous means that both processes must exist simultaneously in order to communicate.

Space Addressing by process identification (task name in Ada, channel name in occam) means that there must be some global scope where processes are defined.

Linda provides *uncoupling* in both time and space. This is done by defining a *tuple space* (TS). Tuple space is shared memory, but unlike the computer hardware memory which consists of fixed size words, TS consists of *tuples* which are typed sequences of data. Tuples are rather like parameter lists of procedures which define a fixed length sequence of typed objects. Every call to the same procedure uses the same parameter signature, though different procedures may have different signatures.[1]

The concurrent programming primitives of Linda work by pattern matching on the tuple signatures. None of the following tuples will match because their signatures are different:

---

[1] Even if some form of variable parameter lists are provided for the procedure call, like the default parameters in Ada, the called procedure will have an identifiable signature.

110

- (1,'A') - (integer, character)
- (1, 2) - (integer, integer)
- ('A',1) - (character, integer)

The primitives of Linda are:

Output(T) Add the tuple T to the tuple space.

Input(T) Remove a matching tuple T from the tuple space. If there is no matching tuple, suspend until one does match.

Read(T) Like Input(T), but do not remove the tuple.

Try_Input(T) Non-blocking version of Input. If a matching tuple does not exist, continue.

Try_Read(R) Non-blocking version of Read.

The power of the Linda primitives comes from the fact that tuples may contain formal elements. Again to make the analogy with procedures, a procedure declaration contains declarations of formal parameters which are variables while a procedure call contains actual parameters which are values that are transferred to the formal parameters. Linda can emulate a simple procedure call by having actual parameters in a tuple placed in the TS and formal parameters in the tuple used in the Input statement.

```
Output(1, 'A');
```

```
Input(I: Integer; C: Character);
```

The Input statement would suspend until the Output statement has added its tuple to the TS. Then it would match the signature and remove the tuple from TS, copying its values into the formal 'parameters' I and C. If a Read primitive were used, the process would still suspend until the tuple was added to the TS and the tuple values would be copied to the 'parameters', but the tuple would remain in the TS. There are non-blocking versions of these primitives but they will not be used in the examples in this book.

Linda is more flexible than it would seem from a cursory examination, because there is no restriction that the tuples in TS be value-tuples only. The Output statement can place tuples with formal elements in the TS which can be matched by values in an Input statement. For example, Figure 10.1 shows how a process can specify that a request be served by a specific process, or by any process that chooses to match the tuple. The tuples have three elements:

1. A string identifying this tuple as a job request.
2. An integer identifying the job to be done.
3. A name identifying the process ID.

The Input statement is issued by process 24 to indicate that it is ready to accept any job. The first Output statement requests that job number 17 be done only by process 24, while the second Output statement places a tuple with a formal process ID in the TS. *Any* process will be able to match the tuple.

The next example shows how a remote procedure call or simple Ada rendezvous (Figure 10.2) may be programmed in Linda (Figure 10.3). The first two

```
Input ("job", J: Job_ID, 24);      -- process 24 waits to serve

Output("job", 17, 24);             -- send request to process 24

Output("job", 17, P: Process_ID); -- send request to any process
```
Figure 10.1 Tuples in Linda

lines are executed by the calling process which adds to the TS a tuple containing the following fields:

1. A string containing the name of the remote procedure.
2. The name of the calling process.
3. Two input parameters (an integer and a character).

The first line adds the tuple to the TS and the second waits for the completion of the remote procedure.

```
accept Proc(I: in  Integer;
            C: in  Character;
            B: out Boolean) do
    ...
end Proc;

Proc(65, 'X', B);   -- call to entry
```
Figure 10.2 Ada rendezvous to be simulated

```
-- code for calling process
  Output("Proc", 24, 65, 'X');
  Input (24, B: Boolean);

-- code for accepting process
  Input("Proc", Caller: Process_ID, I: Integer, C: Character);
  Proc(I, C, B);
  Output(Caller, B);
```
Figure 10.3 Linda simulation of rendezvous

The next three lines are executed by the process containing the remote procedure. The first line waits for the call by matching on the name of the procedure and then copies the parameters while removing the tuple. The second line executes the procedure using the two input parameters and returns a result parameter (a boolean value). The third line adds a tuple to the TS containing the process ID of the caller and the value of the result parameter. These can now be matched by the **Input** statement in the calling process, which will copy the result parameter and release itself from suspension.

The important point to learn from this example is that the calling process and the called process are uncoupled in space and time. Neither need know the name of the other (the process ID is only passed as a parameter at run time) and in fact, neither process need even be in existence when the other reaches the 'rendezvous' point, the initial matching Input and Output.

10.2 Matrix Multiplication in Linda

The Linda program for matrix multiplication demonstrates the preferred paradigm of programming in this language just as the same problem did for occam. In the case of Linda, the solution contains absolutely no information as to the number of processes involved, unlike the occam solution with its clearly defined process topology.

Figure 10.4 is the main process of the program whose task is to initialize the tuple space with the rows of the first matrix and the columns of the second. Then the process adds to the tuple space a 'next job counter' called Next with initial value 1. Finally, it loops on an Input statement 'reaping' result tuples as they are added to the TS.

```
Output('A', 1, (1,2,3));    -- Rows of first matrix
Output('A', 2, (4,5,6));
Output('A', 3, (7,8,9));
Output('B', 1, (1,0,2));    -- Columns of second matrix
Output('B', 2, (1,2,1));
Output('B', 3, (1,1,1));

Output("Next", 1);          -- Next job counter

for I in 1..3 loop          -- Loop to reap results
  for J in 1..3 loop
    Input('C', I, J: Integer, C: Integer);
    -- Print C(I,J)
  end loop;
end loop;
```

Figure 10.4 Matrix multiplication – main process

The actual work of the matrix multiplication is done by *worker processes* (Figure 10.5). Each such process takes the job counter from the TS, and returns it to the TS after incrementing the value. The value of the counter is the element of the result array that needs to be computed. The row and column whose multiplication gives this result element can be easily computed. For example, the fourth element needs the first column and the second row. The equation for an array element is $element = (row - 1) * 3 + col$ which gives $4 = (2 - 1) * 3 + 1$ in this case. The row and column of the two input matrices are obtained from the TS using Read rather than Input since the data must remain for computing the other elements. Finally, the result tuple is added to the TS.

Clearly, this program remains identical no matter how many worker processes are computing concurrently. There are nine multiplications to be performed and

```
task body Workers is
  -- local data declarations
begin
  loop
    Input("Next", Element);          -- Get job number
    Output("Next", Element+1);       -- Put next job number
    exit when Element > 3 * 3;       -- Check for termination
    I := (Element - 1)  /  3 + 1;    -- Compute row number
    J := (Element - 1) mod 3 + 1;    -- Compute column number
    Row_Tuple := Read('A', I, V1);   -- Get row
    Col_Tuple := Read('B', J, V2);   -- Get column
    X := Inner_Product(V1, V2);      -- Compute result
    Output('C', I, J, X);            -- Put result
  end loop;
end Workers;
```

Figure 10.5 Matrix multiplication – worker processes

it does not matter whether there are nine workers or just one. The only possible effect is in the performance of the program. No modification is necessary to the program text.

This can be seen by looking at a possible declaration of the processes as Ada tasks (Figure 10.6). Two static worker tasks are declared, but we could just as well decide at execution time how many tasks to allocate. A final advantage to the Linda solution is that the solution is robust even if the processes execute on several different processors of varying performance. We could have two fast processors and two slow processors. Then two-thirds of the work would be done by the fast processors and one-third by the slow ones. This should be contrasted with the occam solution which assumes a fixed topology of identical processors.

```
task type Workers;              -- task type
W: array (1..2) of Workers;     -- Two static processes

procedure Work(N: Workers) is
  W: array(1..N) of Workers     -- Allocate number of
begin                           --    workers at run time
  -- wait for termination
end Work; .
```

Figure 10.6 Declaration of worker tasks

To summarize, the Linda formalism uses an extremely powerful, but simple, primitive to give unparalleled expressiveness and flexibility, though there is obviously a price to be paid in efficiency. The implementation of Linda is discussed in Chapter 15.

10.3 Further Reading

Gelernter's original article [Gel85] on Linda is the source of most of the examples. The matrix multiplication example is from [ACG86]. A recent description of programming style in Linda is [CG89].

Chapter 11

Distributed Mutual Exclusion

11.1 Introduction

The previous chapters in Part II described formalisms that are appropriate for distributed programming. This chapter begins the study of distributed algorithms by presenting a solution to the mutual exclusion problem. We will distinguish between *nodes* and *processes*. A node is a physically identifiable object which may contain several concurrent processes. The internal synchronization among processes in a node is accomplished using common-memory primitives while processes in different nodes can communicate only by sending and receiving messages.

The model used is the following:

1. Each node has a two-way communications channel with each other node.
2. The communications channels are error-free.
3. The transit times of messages are finite but arbitrary. In particular, messages need not be delivered in order.
4. Nodes do not fail.

The last assumption is stronger than the one we used for solving mutual exclusion in common-memory models. There a process was allowed to fail during execution of its non-critical section. Here a node must not fail because the mutual exclusion will be accomplished by a co-operative protocol. Actually, the requirement is somewhat weaker. A node may fail in the sense of remaining forever in its non-critical section. It is only required that the node continue to execute underlying processes that send and receive messages.

11.2 Outline of the Algorithm

The algorithm is based on sequence numbers like the bakery algorithm. However, since the nodes cannot directly read the internal variables of the other nodes, the comparison of sequence numbers and the decision to enter the critical section must be made by sending and receiving messages. The basic idea is the same: a node chooses a number, broadcasts its choice to the other nodes (a *Request* message) and then waits until it has received confirmation (a *Reply*) from each other node that the number chosen is now the lowest outstanding sequence number. Ties on the chosen sequence number are resolved arbitrarily in favor of the node with the lowest identification number.

The structure of the algorithm for one node is shown in Figure 11.1. There are three processes:

1.   The main process which executes the usual loop of protocols enclosing a critical section.
2.   A process which receives *Request* messages from other nodes.
3.   A process which receives *Reply* messages from other nodes.

A node which receives a *Request* from another node must respond with its sequence number. The node compares the received number with its own. If the received

```
task body Main_Process_Type is
begin
  loop
    Non_Critical_Section;        -- Pre-protocol
    Choose_Sequence_Number;      --      "
    Send_Request_to_Nodes;       --      "
    Wait_for_Reply;              --      "
    Critical_Section;
    Reply_to_Deferred_Nodes;     -- Post-protocol
  end loop;
end Main_Process_Type;

task body Request_Process_Type is
begin
  loop
    accept Message;
    if Decide_to_Defer then
      Defer_Reply;
    else
      Send_Reply;
    end if;
  end loop;
end Request_Process_Type;

task body Reply_Process_Type is
begin
  loop
    accept Message;
    Increment_Reply_Count;
    if Last_Reply then
      Wake_Main_Process;
    end if;
  end loop;
end Reply_Process_Type;
```

Figure 11.1 Structure of the algorithm

number has priority (a lower sequence number) then a reply is sent immediately. If not, the reply is *deferred*. This effectively suspends the sending node in its pre-protocol since it will not enter its critical section until it has received replies from each of the other nodes.

When replies have been received from each of the other nodes, the main process proceeds to execute its critical section. The post-protocol consists of sending the deferred replies, which will eventually release suspended nodes.

11.3   Details of the Algorithm

The three tasks that comprise the mutual exclusion algorithm for each node access global variables that maintain state information about the node (Figure 11.2). These variables are *not* global among the nodes.

Number The sequence number chosen by this node.

High_Number The highest sequence number received so far. Used by the node to choose a higher ticket number.

Requesting A flag to indicate whether this node is requesting its critical section. This is used to skip the comparison of sequence numbers if a node is not contending for the critical section.

Reply_Count Used to count received *Reply* messages so that the node knows when it is allowed to enter its critical section.

S A semaphore to provide mutual exclusion during the access to these global variables by the processes of this node.

Wake_Up A semaphore used to suspend the main process and awaken it when it may proceed to its critical section.

Deferred A data structure indicating which nodes have had their replies deferred.

Finally, N is the number of nodes and I is the node identification. These values are not modified during the execution of the algorithm so they can be compiled constants or values established during initialization.

There must be an underlying communications system that transfers messages from one node to another. We model communications using ordinary rendezvous.

```
Number:        Integer    := 0;
High_Number:   Integer    := 0;
Requesting:    Boolean    := False;
Reply_Count:   Integer    := 0;
S:             Semaphore  := 1;
Wake_Up:       Semaphore  := 0;

Deferred:      array(1..N) of Boolean := (others => False);
```

Figure 11.2 Global variables

```
task type Main_Process_Type;

task type Request_Process_Type is
  entry Message(Num, ID: in Integer);
end Request_Process_Type;

task type Reply_Process_Type is
  entry Message;
end Reply_Process_Type;

Main_Process:    array(1..N) of Main_Process_Type;
Request_Process: array(1..N) of Request_Process_Type;
Reply_Process:   array(1..N) of Reply_Process_Type;
```

Figure 11.3 Declarations for message communications

Each node has access to arrays of tasks (Figure 11.3) so that messages can be sent by a simple entry call indexed by the task index.

The code for the protocol procedures of the main process is shown in Figures 11.4 and 11.5. In Choose_Number the node indicates its desire to enter the critical section and chooses a ticket number. Send_Request sends a message to every other node and initializes Reply_Count which will be used by Reply_Process. Finally, Wait_for_Reply suspends on the semaphore until the node may enter the critical section. The post-protocol resets Requesting and sends *Reply* messages to all deferred nodes.

```
procedure Choose_Number is
begin
  Wait(S);
  Requesting := True;
  Number := High_Number + 1;
  Signal(S);
end Choose_Number;

procedure Send_Request is
begin
  Reply_Count := 0;
  for J in 1..N loop
    if J /= I then
      Request_Process(J).Message(Number, I);
    end if;
  end loop;
end Send_Request;

procedure Wait_for_Reply is
begin
  Wait(Wake_Up);
end Wait_for_Reply;
```

Figure 11.4 Pre-protocol procedures

```
procedure Reply_to_Deferred_Nodes is
begin
  Wait(S);
  Requesting := False;
  Signal(S);
  for J in 1..N loop
    if Deferred(J) then
      Deferred(J) := False;
      Reply_Process(J).Message;
    end if;
  end loop;
end Reply_to_Deferred_Nodes;
```

Figure 11.5 Post-protocol procedures

The task bodies of **Request_Process** and **Reply_Process** are shown in Figures 11.6 and 11.7.   **Request_Process** computes the new highest sequence number received and then makes a decision based on the comparison with the chosen sequence number. **Reply_Process** is straightforward; when replies have been received from all nodes, the main process can be awakened.

The example data in Figure 11.8 may assist in understanding the algorithm. Suppose node 1 has chosen *Number* = 20 and sent **Request**-messages to nodes 2,3

```
task body Request_Process_Type is
  Received_Number: Integer;
  Received_ID:     Integer;
  Decide_to_Defer: Boolean;
begin
  loop
    accept Message(Num, ID: in Integer) do
      Received_Number := Num;
      Received_ID     := ID;
    end Message;
    High_Number := max(High_Number, Received_Number);
    Wait(S);
    Decide_to_Defer := Requesting and
        ( Number < Received_Number or
         (Number = Received_Number and
          I < Received_ID) );
    if Decide_to_Defer then
      Deferred(Received_ID) := True;
    else
      Reply_Process(Received_ID).Message;
    end if;
    Signal(S);
  end loop;
end Request_Process_Type;
```

Figure 11.6 Request process

```
task body Reply_Process_Type is
begin
  loop
    accept Message;
    Reply_Count := Reply_Count + 1;
    if Reply_Count = N - 1 then Signal(Wake_Up); end if;
  end loop;
end Reply_Process_Type;
```

Figure 11.7 Reply process

and 4. Concurrently, nodes 2 and 3 wish to enter their critical sections, choose sequence numbers 23 and 15 respectively, and send Request-messages to all the nodes, in particular, node 1. The request messages cross during transmission.

Based on the result of comparing the sequence numbers, node 1 realizes that node 3 has priority and sends a Reply-message. The reply to node 2 is deferred. Next, it receives a reply from node 4 which apparently is not currently interested in entering the critical section. Then node 2, having received node 1's request, checks sequence numbers and replies. Finally, node 3 completes its critical section and replies to node 1 which may now enter the critical section. Upon exit, the deferred reply to node 2 is sent.

There is nothing unique about the particular interleaving demonstrated. Node 3 could have quickly finished its critical section and replied to node 1 before nodes 2 and 4 reply. This important fact is that a node enters its critical section only if it has received from every other node a reply to its request.

Node	Number	Reply Sent	Reply Received	Event
2	23	No	No	Reply to 3
3	15	Yes	No	
4	-	-	No	
2	23	No	No	Reply from 4
3	15	Yes	No	
4	-	-	Yes	
2	23	No	Yes	Reply from 2
3	15	Yes	No	
4	-	-	Yes	
2	23	No	Yes	Reply from 3
3	15	Yes	Yes	
4	-	-	Yes	
2	23	Yes	Yes	Reply to 2
3	15	Yes	Yes	
4	-	-	Yes	

Figure 11.8 Sample execution

11.4   Correctness of the Algorithm

The algorithm satisfies the mutual exclusion property, does not deadlock and does not starve individual nodes. We will not prove the correctness of the internal processing of each node (which is also a concurrent program) but instead concentrate on the exchange of messages among the nodes.

Theorem 11.4.1 *The algorithm satisfies the mutual exclusion property.*

Proof: The notation and the format of the proof will be modeled on those of the bakery algorithm. We assume that two nodes i and k are in their critical sections simultaneously. Before entering its critical section the last times that i performed certain actions are denoted as follows:

- $write(i)$ – i chose its ticket number
- $send\_req(i)$ – i sent a request to k
- $send\_reply(i)$ – i sent a reply to k
- $receive\_req(k)$ – i received a request from k
- $receive\_reply(k)$ – i received a reply from k

and similarly for k.

With the above notation, the following formulas express obvious relations on the execution of the programs within the nodes:

$$write(i) < send\_req(i) < receive\_reply(k) < at(CS(i))$$
$$write(k) < send\_req(k) < receive\_reply(i) < at(CS(k))$$

In i, there are two cases to consider:

$$receive\_req(k) < write(i)$$
$$write(i) < receive\_req(k)$$

Case 1: $N(i)$ is chosen greater than $N(k)$ and a *Reply* is sent to k. We are not assuming that messages are delivered in the order they are sent, so the *Reply* may arrive before or after the *Request* from i. But in any case k will not send a reply to i until after it has left its critical section as can be seen by checking the three possibilities that can occur in the execution of k:

$$receive\_req(i) < receive\_reply(i) < at(CS(k)) < send\_reply(k)$$
$$receive\_reply(i) < receive\_req(i) < at(CS(k)) < send\_reply(k)$$
$$receive\_reply(i) < at(CS(k)) < receive\_req(i) < send\_reply(k)$$

Case 2: Both nodes first choose a ticket number and only then receive the *Request* message from the other node. Without loss of generality, assume that $N(i) < N(k)$ using node identification numbers to break ties if necessary. Then in node k:

$$send\_reply(k) < receive\_reply(i) < at(CS(k))$$

and in node i:

$$receive\_reply(i) < at(CS(k)) < send\_reply(i)$$

Thus i leaves it critical section before k enters. □

Theorem 11.4.2 *No individual starvation (and hence no deadlock).*

Proof: Suppose that i requests entry to the critical section but never succeeds. Let $ahead(j, i)$ be the set of nodes j such that $Requesting(j) \wedge N(j) < N(i)$. The theorem is proven by induction on the number of nodes in $ahead(j, i)$. First note that the number of such nodes cannot increase because each new requesting node will choose a number greater than $N(i)$.

Let k be the node in $ahead(j, i)$ with the lowest value of $N(j)$. By the assumption on i, it has sent a *Request* message and is waiting for a reply from k. Either k has yet to receive the message or the reply has been deferred.

- If it has yet to receive the message, by comparison of ticket numbers, the reply will be deferred and this case reduces to the other one.

- There are no nodes in $ahead(j, k)$ because then $ahead(j, i)$ for this other node, contradicting the choice of k as the node in $ahead(j, i)$ with the lowest ticket number. Eventually, k must receive replies to all of its requests. It will enter the critical section and upon exit, reply to i.

We have shown that the size of $ahead(j, i)$ never increases and must decrease. By induction, eventually it will be zero and i will enter the critical section. □

11.5 Further Reading

The algorithm in the chapter is from [RA81]. Other algorithms are described in Raynal's survey [Ray86].

11.6 Exercises

1. Prove that the semaphore S is needed. (*Hint:* Interleave the computation of Decide_to_Defer between the two statements in the critical section in Choose_Number).

2. Consider a version of the algorithm obtained by deleting the semaphore S from Reply_to_Deferred_Nodes and moving the Signal(S) in Request_Process_Type before the if-statement. Show that deadlock can occur. (*Hint:* Reply_to_Deferred_Nodes could be interleaved between the computation of Decide_to_Defer and the if-statement).

3. Let a node n send a Reply message to node m and decide to request the critical section by sending *Request* messages to all nodes, in particular to m. Describe the execution sequence if the *Request* message is received by m before the *Reply* message.

4. In a network of N nodes, how many messages are exchanged for each execution of the critical section?

5. (Lamport) Prove the correctness of the following version of the algorithm which explicitly replies to each request rather than deferring a reply which might be interpreted as a lost message. How many messages are exchanged for each execution of the critical section?

   - A node receiving a *Request* message replies with its current ticket number.

   - When a node completes its critical section, it sends a *Release* message with a new (higher) ticket number to all other nodes.

   - A node may enter the critical section if it has received some message with a higher ticket number than its own from every other node.

6. Suppose that there exists an upper bound on message transmission time in the system. Rather than send *Reply* messages, we can send a *Deferred* message and let the absence of a message implicitly indicate a favorable *Reply*. How does this affect the number of messages exchanged?

1ination

s executed its last statement. A
uential processes have terminated.
xecuting infinite loops and do not
nation does exist even in this case
ll waiting for communication from
is is called deadlock.

ent programming, it is trivial to
ready processes is empty. In a
t simple because there is no way
ant of time and then examine it.
iformation from a set of processes
ermination has occurred or not.

irectional communications chan-
messages in the order sent. The
channels can be modeled by two

model is not very restrictive. We do assume the existence of a
unique *source process* which has no incoming edges and from which every process
is accessible along some path (Figure 12.1).

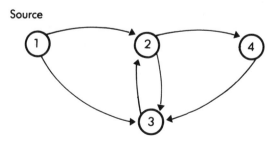

Figure 12.1 Process and channel graph

125

The computation is started when the source process sends a message along each of its outgoing edges. When a process has received its first message, it may commence computation and may send messages along its outgoing edges and receive additional messages from its incoming edges. A process may terminate when its computation is finished. It will send no more messages, but if it receives more messages, it may be restarted. We want to design a signaling scheme to be superimposed on top of the message communications so that when *all* processes have terminated, the source process will eventually be informed.

The signaling will be done on special channels, one for each of the message channels, but pointed in the opposite direction (the dashed lines in Figure 12.2). We will use the term *signals* to distinguish these data from the messages of the main computation. Whatever the status of a process in terms of its computation – which may be terminated, or its message communications channels – which may be blocked, we assume that it is always able to receive, process and send signals.

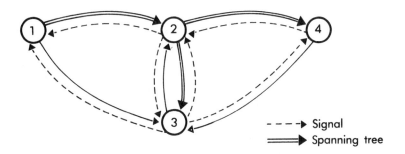

Figure 12.2 Signaling channels and spanning tree

The algorithms will be described within the framework of the Ada program shown in Figure 12.3. There will be a constant number N of nodes each of which runs a task communicating with the outside world. The `Main_Process` doing the computation will be run as a subtask of the `Node` task. The main program is used only for initialization – configuration of the channels and initiation of the nodes. The details are not important here and can be found in Appendix D.

Within each node are declared global variables (Figure 12.4) used to maintain the status of the communications channels and to exchange information between the main process and the underlying communications processing. The variable I is initialized to the node ID and remains constant thereafter. The topology of the the channels is described by the variables `Incoming` and `Outgoing` within each node. `Outgoing(J).Exists` is true if there is a channel from I to J and conversely for `Incoming`. These variables will contain other status fields that differ from one algorithm to the next.

The variables `Received_ID` and `Received_Data` are used to record the information coming from the channels in variables local to the node so that the rendezvous can be completed as soon as possible to free the calling node. Once the rendezvous is completed, the messages and signals are processed. The semaphore

```
with Semaphore_Package; use Semaphore_Package;
procedure Distributed_Algorithm is
  N: constant Integer := 4;

  task type Nodes is
    entry Message(Data: Integer; ID: Integer);
    entry Signal(ID: Integer);
  end Nodes;
  Node: array(1..N) of Nodes;

  task body Nodes is
    -- Global variables

    task Main_Process;
    task body Main_Process is ... ;

  begin
    loop
      select
        accept Message(Data: Integer; ID: Integer) do
          Received_ID := ID;
          Received_Data := Data;
        end Message;
        -- Message processing
      or
        accept Signal(ID: Integer) do
          Received_ID := ID;
        end Signal;
        -- Signal processing
      end select;
    end loop;
  end Nodes;
begin
  -- Configure nodes and initiate processes
end Distributed_Algorithm;
```

Figure 12.3 Framework for distributed algorithms

S is used to protect global variables that may be used by both the Main_Process and the Node process.

12.2 The Dijkstra–Scholten Algorithm

If the process graph were structured as a tree, a simple algorithm would suffice to determine termination. A leaf process would decide that it has terminated and send a signal to its parent process. When a process has received notification from all its child processes, it sends a signal to its parent, and so on until the source process is informed. The Ada language has a scheme for termination defined within the language that is based the fact that task dependencies form a tree.

```
type Edge is
  record
    Exists:  Boolean := False;
    -- Other fields
  end record;

Incoming: array(1..N) of Edge;
Outgoing: array(1..N) of Edge;

I:             Integer;
S:             Binary_Semaphore := Init(1);
Received_ID:   Integer;
Received_Data: Integer;
```

Figure 12.4 Global variables for distributed algorithms

The algorithm can be extended to acyclic directed process graphs as follows. An additional field `Deficit` is added to each edge. On incoming edges this will denote the difference between the number of messages received and the number of signals sent in reply. When a node wishes to terminate, it sends enough signals to ensure that the deficit is zero on each incoming edge. Then it waits until it has received signals from outgoing edges reducing their deficits to zero. As a simplification, a single counter `N_Signals` is sufficient since the requirement is only that all outgoing deficits are zero and no part of the algorithm depends on the identity of the channel from which the signals are received.

If cycles are allowed, the above algorithm fails because we have no leaf processes that can decide to terminate without consulting other processes. The Dijkstra–Scholten (DS) algorithm solves this problem by generating a *spanning tree* during the exchange of messages and then using the tree to order the signals. A spanning tree (Figure 12.2) is a subset of the edges of the graph that forms a tree such that every node is incident with an edge in the tree. The tree will be directed with the source process at its root.

A variable `First_Edge` is added to each node which implicitly creates a spanning tree: the first time that a message is received in a process, the incoming edge upon which the message is received will be added to the tree. Termination requires three steps:

1. Send signals on all incoming edges *except* `First_Edge`.
2. Wait for signals from all outgoing edges.
3. Send signals on `First_Edge`.

The algorithm is shown in Figures 12.5–12.8. Figure 12.6 shows additional processing that must be done by the `Node` process when it receives a message or a signal. The first time that a message is received along any edge `First_Edge` is set. In any case, the deficit is incremented. If a signal is received, the number of outstanding signals is decremented.

If `Main_Process` wishes to send a message, it executes the procedure shown in Figure 12.7 incrementing the signal count.

```
type Edge is
  record
    Exists:  Boolean := False;
    Deficit: Integer := 0;
  end record;

N_Signals:  Integer := 0;
First_Edge: Integer := 0;
```

Figure 12.5 Global variables for termination (DS)

```
-- Message processing
  if First_Edge = 0 then
    First_Edge := Received_ID;
  end if;
  Wait(S);
  Incoming(Received_ID).Deficit :=
    Incoming(Received_ID).Deficit + 1;
  Signal(S);

-- Signal processing
  Wait(S);
  N_Signals := N_Signals - 1;
  Signal(S);
```

Figure 12.6 Receiving messages and signals (DS)

The essence of the algorithm is in the function Decide_to_Terminate (Figure 12.8) which Main_Process executes when it has no more processing to do. Signals are sent on incoming edges (except First_Edge). If there are no outstanding signals to be received on outgoing edges, signals are sent on First_Edge and we can terminate. The coding of the function is somewhat convoluted by the desire to protect variables that are global to both processes in the node while at the same time not calling another node from within a critical section since that could lead to deadlock.

The creation of the spanning tree may be traced in the example in Figure 12.2, where the double lines define the spanning tree. This tree would be produced by node 1 initiating the computation by sending a message to node 2 which would relay it to nodes 3 and 4. The tree is not unique and a different sequence of

```
procedure Send_Message(Data: Integer; ID: Integer) is
begin
  Wait(S);
  N_Signals := N_Signals + 1;
  Signal(S);
  Node(ID).Message(Data, I);
end Send_Message;
```

Figure 12.7 Sending messages (DS)

```
function Decide_to_Terminate return Boolean is
  procedure Send_Signals(ID: Integer) is
  begin
    while Incoming(ID).Deficit > 0 loop
      Incoming(ID).Deficit := Incoming(ID).Deficit - 1;
      Signal(S);
      Node(ID).Signal(I);
      Wait(S);
    end loop;
  end Send_Signals;

begin
  for J in 1..N loop
    if  J /= First_Edge then
      Wait(S);
      Send_Signals(J);
      Signal(S);
    end if;
  end loop;

  Wait(S);
  if N_Signals = 0 then
    if I /= 1 and First_Edge /= 0 then
      Send_Signals(First_Edge);
      First_Edge := 0;
    end if;
    Signal(S);
    return True;
  else
    Signal(S);
    return False;
  end if;
end Decide_to_Terminate;
```

Figure 12.8 Algorithm for termination (DS)

messages would build a different tree. For example, if node 4 sent message to 3 and it arrived at 3 before the message from 2 then the edge 4 → 3 would be in the spanning tree instead of 2 → 3.

Note that we do not wait for outstanding signals within the function. The reason is that additional *messages* may be received on the incoming edges which will cause the computation in Main_Process to be restarted. The final state of this algorithm is that source process reports termination of the system while the other processes are quiescent in the sense that no node is computing within Main_Process. However, the underlying communications process in Node has no way of knowing whether the entire system has terminated or whether only this node is temporarily without work until a new message arrives. Thus it must continually check for incoming messages. In the next section, we will modify the algorithm to enable all processes to terminate.

The correctness properties of this algorithm are:

Safety If the program decides that termination has occurred, then all processes are quiescent.

Liveness If all processes become quiescent then eventually the program decides to terminate.

For each node, let $D = \sum Deficit$ where the sum is taken over all incoming edges. We leave as an exercise the proof of the following theorem:

Theorem 12.2.1 *The following formulas are invariants in each node:*

$$D \geq 0 \tag{12.1}$$

$$N\_Signals \geq 0 \tag{12.2}$$

$$D > 0 \vee N\_Signals = 0 \tag{12.3}$$

Define an *engaged* process as one that has received a message and has not yet become quiescent. Note that processes may become engaged several times and that processes that are disengaged continue to send and receive signals. Define an *engagement* edge as an edge that is a First_Edge for some node.

Theorem 12.2.2 *The following statements are invariant:*
1. *An engagement edge has non-zero deficit.*
2. *The engagement edges form a tree.*
3. *Every engaged node is reachable from the source node by a directed path formed from engagement edges.*

The program announces termination only if the tree is degenerate and consists only of the source node. Safety of the algorithm follows since the theorem implies that all other nodes are not engaged.

Liveness follows by induction on the height of the tree. If a leaf terminates, it will signal First_Edge because it is not waiting for signals on any outgoing edge. For other nodes, the result follows using the termination of the subtrees as an inductive hypothesis.

12.3 Termination using Markers

As noted in the previous section, the main process cannot assume that if it is quiescent it may terminate. In effect, the communications task is buffering the incoming messages. With buffered channels, we have to ensure that the channels are empty before terminating. On a distributed system, this can be difficult. In Figure 12.9(a) process P2 will note that the channel is empty and may decide to terminate. Then process P1 sends the message (Figure 12.9(b)) and also decides to terminate since it has nothing left to do. The outstanding message which should have caused P2 to continue execution is lost.

Figure 12.9 Disappearing message

To solve this problem, we must be able to account for all messages so that an empty message channel can be correctly identified. The following termination with marking (TM) algorithm sends special *marker* messages to indicate that a channel has become empty. The source process will initiate checking for termination by sending a marker on its outgoing edges. When a process decides to terminate, it first waits for markers on all incoming edges (if they have not already arrived) and then propagates a copy of the marker message along all outgoing edges. Once a process has received markers from all incoming edges, it can proceed as before: it signals all incoming edges except the first one and waits for signals on the outgoing edges before signaling the first edge.

The TM algorithm is shown in Figures 12.10–12.13. The marker is denoted by a negative integer message. An additional simplification has been made in this algorithm by maintaining a boolean variable for `Active` channels instead of computing non-zero deficits. Incoming edges have an additional field denoting whether a marker has been received or not.

```
type Edge is
  record
    Exists:           Boolean := False;
    Active:           Boolean := False;
    Marker_Received:  Boolean := False;
  end record;
```

Figure 12.10 Global variables for TM algorithm

Message and signal processing (Figures 12.11 and 12.12) are similar to the previous algorithm except for the use of the `Active` field rather than deficits. The modifications to `Decide_to_Terminate` are immediate and left as an exercise.

The main difference is in `Main_Process`, a fragment of which is shown in Figure 12.13 (the complete listing is given in Appendix D). We do not even attempt to terminate before receiving a marker from `First_Edge`. Then markers are sent to all outgoing edges and we wait until markers have been received on all incoming edges. Only now are we assured that the channels are empty and we can commence the sending and receiving signals to collapse the spanning tree.

```
-- Message processing
 if Received_Data < 0 then
   Incoming(Received_ID).Marker_Received := True;
 else
   if First_Edge = 0 then
     First_Edge := Received_ID;
   end if;
 end if;
 if not Incoming(Received_ID).Active then
   Incoming(Received_ID).Active := True;
 end if;

-- Signal processing
 Outgoing(Received_ID).Active := False;
 Wait(S);
 N_Signals := N_Signals - 1;
 Signal(S);
```

Figure 12.11 Receiving messages and signals (TM)

```
procedure Send_Message(Data: Integer; ID: Integer) is
begin
  if not Outgoing(ID).Active then
    Outgoing(ID).Active := True;
    Wait(S);
    N_Signals := N_Signals + 1;
    Signal(S);
  end if;
  Node(ID).Message(Data, I);
end Send_Message;
```

Figure 12.12 Sending messages (TM)

12.4   Snapshots

The TM algorithm is a special case of a more general algorithm that can capture the global state of a system — a *distributed snapshot*. The state of a node will be

```
loop
    exit when Incoming(First_Edge).Marker_Received;
end loop;

-- send markers to all outgoing edges

loop
  exit when Markers_Received;
end loop;

loop
  exit when Decide_to_Terminate;
end loop;
```

Figure 12.13 Main process (TM)

defined as the sequence of messages that have been sent and received along all channels incident with the node. The state of a channel will be the sequence of messages transmitted to the channel but not yet delivered.

The source process initiates the algorithm by recording its state and sending a marker on outgoing channels before any more messages are sent. Upon the first receipt of a marker, a receiving process records its state, records the state of that channel as empty and propagates the marker. At any time after recording its state, if a process receives a marker from another incoming edge, it records the state of that channel as the sequence of messages received between the state it recorded and the receipt of the marker. Figure 12.14 shows the system immediately after

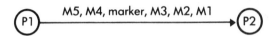

Figure 12.14 Distributed snapshots

P2 has recorded its state. Messages $M1, M2, M3$ received before the marker, are determined by P2 to be part of the state of the channel for this snapshot. Messages $M4, M5$ received after the marker, were sent after P1 recorded its state and thus are not part of the state of the channel.

The algorithm is very flexible and only requires that every node be reachable from some node that spontaneously decides to record the state. In fact, several nodes could concurrently decide to record the state and the algorithm would still succeed.

An implementation of the snapshot algorithm is shown in Figures 12.15–12.17. The data structures are shown in Figure 12.15. Last_Message keeps track of the

```
type Edge is
  record
    Exists:         Boolean := False;
    Last_Message:   Integer := 0;
    Recorded_State: Integer := 0;
    Marker_State:   Integer := -1;
  end record;

State_Recorded:  Boolean := False;
```

Figure 12.15 Global variables for snapshot algorithm

number of the last message received or sent on that edge. The current state of a node is defined as the values of the Last_Message field for all incoming and outgoing edges. To record the state of a node, we record the current value of Last_Message in the field Recorded_State.

Recording the state of a channel is the resposibility of the receiving process. For each incoming edge, an additional field Marker_State records the value of Last_Message when the marker is received. The state of the channel is the difference between Marker_State and Recorded_State. If the state of the node is recorded *before* a marker has been received on some channel, `Recorded_State` may be less than `Marker_State` and their difference denotes messages that were sent before the transmitting node recorded its state but received only after the target node recorded its state. Message reception is shown in Figure 12.16. Receipt

```
-- Message processing
  if Received_Data < 0 then
    if Incoming(Received_ID).Marker_State < 0 then
      Incoming(Received_ID).Marker_State :=
        Incoming(Received_ID).Last_Message;
    if not State_Recorded then Record_State; end if;
    end if;
  else
    Wait(S);
    Incoming(Received_ID).Last_Message := Received_Data;
    Signal(S);
  end if;
```

Figure 12.16 Receiving messages (snapshot)

of a message causes `Last_Message` to be updated. The first receipt of a marker causes `Marker_State` to be recorded. A negative value is used as a flag to indicate that a marker has yet to be received. If the state has not yet been recorded, `Record_State` is called.

Sending a message is similar (Figure 12.17). A message causes `Last_Message`

```
procedure Send_Message(Data: Integer; ID: Integer) is
begin
  Wait(S);
  Outgoing(ID).Last_Message := Data;
  Signal(S);
  Node(ID).Message(Data, I);
end Send_Message;

procedure Send_Markers is
begin
  for J in All_Outgoing_Edges  loop
    Wait(S);
    Outgoing(J).Recorded_State := Outgoing(J).Last_Message;
    Signal(S);
    Node(J).Message(-1, I);
  end loop;
end Send_Markers;
```

Figure 12.17 Sending messages (snapshot)

to be updated and a marker causes `Recorded_State` to be updated.

`Record_State` (Figure 12.18) may be called by either the main process when it spontaneously records its state or by **accept** `Message` upon receipt of a message.

It records the state of the incoming edges and then sends markers on all outgoing edges which will cause the state of these edges to be recorded.

```
procedure Record_State is
begin
    Wait(S);
    for J in 1..N loop
      if Incoming(J).Exists then
        Incoming(J).Recorded_State := Incoming(J).Last_Message;
      end if;
    end loop;
    Signal(S);
    Send_Markers;
    State_Recorded := True;
end Record_State;
```

Figure 12.18 Recording the state (snapshot)

The snapshot algorithm was run on the graph of Figure 12.1 where nine messages were sent along each channel. Node 1 decided to record the state after sending six messages and node 4 independently decided to record the state after sending three messages. Upon termination, the results as collected from each node are shown in Figure 12.19. Node 2 sent four messages on each of the two outgoing channels to nodes 3 and 4. Node 3 received three messages before recording its state leaving only the fourth message to be associated with the channel. Node 4 received messages 1 through 2 and recorded that messages 3 and 4 were in transit. The reader should check the snapshot for consistency - each message sent was either received at the target node or recorded as being in transit in the channel.

12.5   Further Reading

The Dijkstra–Scholten algorithm is from [DS80]. Termination by marking uses ideas from [MC82] and [CL85]. The latter paper is the source of the snapshot algorithm.

12.6   Exercises

1. How many spanning trees are there for the example in Figure 12.1? Describe execution sequences to construct each one.

2. Prove theorems 12.2.1 and 12.2.2.

3. Prove the liveness of the DS algorithm.

4. Suppose that an internal node in the DS algorithm terminates if Decide_to_Terminate is true. Create a scenario demonstrating incorrect behavior of the algorithm caused by a message sent but never received.

```
Node  1
      Outgoing channels
         2 sent  1.. 6
         3 sent  1.. 6
      Incoming  channels
Node  2
      Outgoing channels
         3 sent  1.. 4
         4 sent  1.. 4
      Incoming  channels
         1 received 1.. 4 stored  5.. 6
         3 received 1.. 8
Node  3
      Outgoing channels
         2 sent  1.. 8
      Incoming  channels
         1 received 1.. 3 stored  4..  6
         2 received 1.. 3 stored  4..  4
         4 received 1.. 3
Node  4
      Outgoing channels
         3 sent  1.. 3
      Incoming  channels
         2 received 1.. 2 stored  3..  4
```

Figure 12.19 An example of a snapshot

5. What changes need to be made to `Decide_to_Terminate` of the DS algorithm to use it in the TM algorithm?

6. In the TM algorithm, what is the purpose of the `Active` field in outgoing edges?

7. Can a `Main_Process` of the TM algorithm initiate termination upon receipt of a marker from any incoming edge or does it have to be `First_Edge`?

8. Consider an algorithm like the DS algorithm but using `Active` fields like the TM algorithm rather than deficits. What could happen? (*Hint:* consider the scenario in Figure 12.20.)

9. Can `Recorded_State` equal `Last_Message` even if the state is spontaneously recorded before a marker has been received?

10. Describe a scenario demonstrating a bug in the implementation of the snapshot algorithm. (*Hint:* If `Record_State` is called by `accept Message`, the main process could interleave calls to `Send_Message` between recording the state and the actual transmission of the marker.)

11. Create extreme scenarios for the snapshot algorithm: one with all channels empty and one with all channels full.

- Node 2 sends message to node 4.

- Node 4 receives message from 2.

- Node 2 sends message to node 4.

- Node 4 sends signal to 2.

- Node 4 receives message from 2.

- Node 2 receives signal from 4.

- Node 4 sends signal to 2.

- Node 2 receives signal from 4.

Figure 12.20 Scenario for DS with `Active` fields

Chapter 13

The Byzantine Generals Problem

13.1 Introduction

Distributed processing is used not only to create faster systems by exploiting parallelism but also to improve reliability by replicating a computation in several processors. Such a system attempts to be *fault tolerant*, that is to continue to produce correct, or at least reasonable, results even if some components fail. A distributed system is not automatically fault tolerant. Our algorithm for distributed mutual exclusion requires the co-operation of all the processes and will deadlock if one of them fails.

A typical architecture for a fault-tolerant system is shown in Figure 13.1(a). The data from input sensors are replicated along a bus. Several processors each compute the required output. Special circuits compare the values using majority voting and control the outputs. If only one processor malfunctions, it will not affect the output. The computers will be interconnected so that the faulty processor can identified and the system operator notified. In very critical systems like flight controllers, the input sensors and output controllers will also be replicated as shown in Figure 13.1(b).

There are several serious difficulties that must be overcome in designing a fault-tolerant system:

1. When the input sensors are replicated, they may not all give *exactly* the same data. Voting on the outcome is no longer a trivial comparison of two digital values. Even if the difference is physically negligible, the computational algorithms must be designed so that neighboring input values give answers that are near each other.

2. A faulty input sensor or processor may not act 'nicely'. They may produce spurious data or values that are totally out of the range considered by the algorithms.

3. Even if the hardware is not faulty, if all processors are using the same software then system is not fault-tolerant of software bugs. If several different programs are used, they may give slightly different values on the same data. Worse, different programmers are prone to make the same misinterpretations of the program specifications.

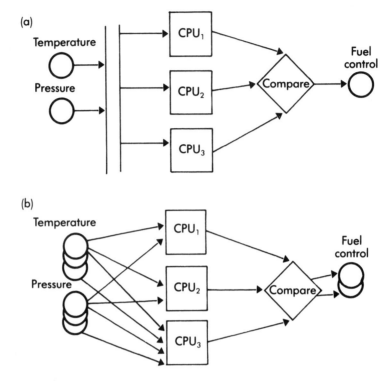

Figure 13.1 Architectures for fault-tolerant systems

The Byzantine Generals problem is an abstraction of one problem encountered in designing reliable systems. As usual we define a specific model and discuss the existence (or non-existence) of algorithms to solve the problem in this model. The applicability of the algorithm depends on the applicability of the model and the willingness of the designer to pay for the overhead of the solution. Solutions under other models can be found in the research literature.

13.2   Description of the Problem

In some of our solutions to the mutual exclusion problem, we allowed a process to die gracefully – it was supposed to terminate in its non-critical section after resetting the protocol variables to a non-interfering value. We indicated that the solutions fail if a process is allowed to fail in its critical section and this is obviously true if a process can assign arbitrary values to the protocol variables. The Byzantine Generals problem considers the situation where faulty processes are actively 'traitorous' and can send any message to the other processes.

A set of units of the Byzantine army is preparing for action against an enemy. Each unit is commanded by a general and these generals communicate with each other by sending messages over telephone lines. The properties of the telephones are as follows:

1. The lines are error free. More than that, no general can interfere with a telephone line connecting two other generals.

2. The lines are point-to-point like occam channels and thus the sender is unequivocally identified to the receiver.

3. The telephone operators are in constant contact so that the absence of a message means that the sender did not send one and not that the enemy cut the line.

The purpose of these restrictions is to initially limit the problem to coping with the contents of the messages and not with other forms of faults.

The generals must agree on a course of action. Let us assume that this can be described by deciding between simple pre-arranged alternatives like: 'attack' or 'retreat', or 'attack on left' or 'attack on right'. The algorithm must satisfy the following two properties:

1. All loyal generals must take the same decision.

2. Every loyal general must base his decision on correct information from every other loyal general.

The first property means that the enemy cannot divide the Byzantine army simply by having a few traitors issue messages. The second property means that the algorithm used by the loyal generals cannot be random but has to be based on what the other loyal generals actually think.

To see the motivation behind this abstraction, consider an aircraft collision avoidance system with four processors. To ensure that the system is not accidentally engaged, three processors must agree on a course of action. If a collision is impending, the processors should be able to agree to automatically turn the aircraft left or right depending on the position of the other aircraft. It should not be possible for one faulty processor to send messages to the functioning processors that would cause them to split two against one on the proposed course of action and thus fail to engage the system. Furthermore, if all three processors conclude that a right turn is the best maneuver, they should agree to turn right. The faulty processor is not allowed even to have them all agree to turn left. Only if the computation is so close that either left or right would be correct, could the faulty processor influence the decision.

If more than two-thirds of the generals are loyal, there is a solution, that is, an algorithm that will cause them all to take the same action regardless of what messages are received from the traitorous generals. However, if one-third or more of the generals are traitorous, it can be shown that there is no algorithm to solve the problem. In the case of one traitorous general, there is a solution for four generals and none for three. We will describe the algorithm and the impossibility proof for this particular case in the next two sections.

13.3   Algorithm for Four Generals

There are three loyal generals and one traitor. We assume that all the loyal generals follow the same algorithm, in particular that they inform every other general of their proposed plan of action. The communications channel is assumed to be error-free. The absence of a message is detectable, so we assume that every general, even the traitorous ones, sends the messages required by the following algorithm.

Let one of the generals initiate the algorithm. This general will be called the *commander* and the other generals will be called *lieutenants*. The algorithm is as follows:

1. The commander sends his decision.

2. A lieutenant relays the commander's decision to every other lieutenant.

3. Upon receiving both the direct message from the commander and the relayed messages from the other two lieutenants, the lieutenant decides by majority voting on the three messages.

There are two cases to be considered – either the commander is loyal (Figure 13.2) or he is a traitor (Figure 13.3). If the commander is loyal, his decision to attack is presumed to be the correct decision and we must show that both loyal lieutenants make the same decision. In the figure we can see that a loyal lieutenant receives *attack* from the commander and *also* from the other loyal lieutenant. The traitor may send either *attack* or *retreat*, but by majority voting it cannot affect the outcome.

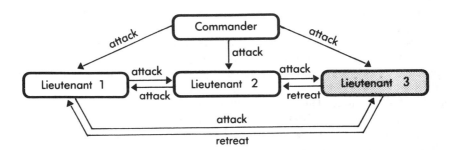

Figure 13.2 Algorithm with loyal commander

If the commander is a traitor, it does not matter what he decides to do as long as the three lieutenants agree on a course of action. Since all lieutenants are loyal, they all correctly relay the commander's message. Thus all three lieutenants receive exactly the same three messages. Thus whatever algorithm they use, they will all take the same decision. In the figure we have shown the commander sending one *attack* message, on *retreat* message and refraining from sending any message to lieutenant 3. If the algorithm agreed upon treats the absence of a message as *attack*, all three lieutenants will attack. Obviously, if the commander sent two or three lieutenants the same message, the majority voting would lead to agreement.

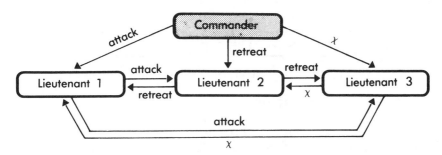

Figure 13.3 Algorithm with traitorous commander

13.4 Impossibility for Three Generals

The above solution does not work for three generals, one of whom is a traitor and in fact, it can be proven that there is no such solution. Suppose that the commander is loyal and that he sends *attack* messages (Figure 13.4). The loyal lieutenant will receive *attack* from the commander and some message, say *retreat*, from the traitorous lieutenant. Since the commander is loyal, the lieutenant must be using some algorithm that causes him to decide to attack.

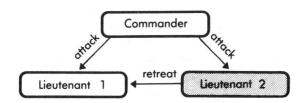

Figure 13.4 Impossibility with loyal commander

On the other hand, if the commander is a traitor, he could send *attack* to lieutenant 1 and *retreat* to lieutenant 2 who will faithfully relay it to lieutenant 1 (Figure 13.5). The situations are indistinguishable from the point of view of lieutenant 1, so whatever decision he takes in the first case he must also take in the second case. So he decides to attack.

A symmetrical argument shows that if a lieutenant receives a *retreat* message from the commander, he must retreat. Thus in the second case, loyal lieutenant 2 will decide to retreat which is not in agreement with lieutenant 1.

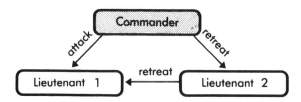

Figure 13.5 Impossibility with traitorous commander

13.5 Further Reading

The Byzantine Generals problem and the results here are from [LSP82]. Books on fault-tolerant computing are [Pra86] and [Shr85]. [SG84] describes how the first launch of the Space Shuttle was delayed because of a fault in the synchronization between the main computer and the backup computer. This example shows that fault-tolerant systems are more complex and will have more faults than an ordinary system but the faults that do occur will not be as catastrophic.

13.6 Exercises

Let us construct a solution to the Byzantine Generals problem in the presence of two traitors.

- The commander sends his decision to each of the $n-1$ lieutenants. Call this a level-2 value.
- Each lieutenant i sends the level-2 value he received to each of the $n-2$ other lieutenants. Call this a level-1 value $v(i)$.
- Each lieutenant k sends the level-1 value he received $v(j)$ to each of the $n-3$ other lieutenants. Call this a level-0 value $v(j)(k)$.
- Eventually, each lieutenant i receives $n-2$ values for lieutenant j: one level-1 value $v(j)$ and $n-2$ level-0 values $v(j)(k)$. By majority vote, lieutenant i can determine a value for lieutenant j.
- Using the $n-2$ values obtained for the other lieutenants in the previous step and the level-2 value from the commander, lieutenant i makes his decision by majority vote.

1. Show that the above algorithm is correct for seven generals and two traitors. (*Hint:* If the commander is loyal, a lieutenant will have four level-0 values and one level-1 value to determine the value for each other lieutenant. But at most two of the five can come from traitors. If the commander is a traitor, five out of six lieutenants are loyal and it is easy to show that they all compute the same value.)

2. Show that the above algorithm is not correct for six generals and two traitors. (*Hint:* A lieutenant obtains only four values from which to compute the value for each other lieutenant. Majority voting cannot help.)

PART III

Implementation Principles

Chapter 14

Single Processor Implementation

14.1 Introduction

Concurrent programming can be implemented by sharing the computational resources of a single processor. We review the resources required to execute a single process and then show how to implement concurrency.

Compilation of a program produces an object program which is stored in memory. The program is executed by a processor which fetches instructions from memory and then executes the computation indicated by the instruction. An *instruction pointer* (IP) keeps track of the current instruction being executed. When an instruction has been executed, the IP is incremented[1] unless the instruction is a jump or procedure call which explicitly modifies the IP. Most instructions read or write memory locations (aside from the object code itself). Additional resources such as general registers or I/O channels can be treated similar to the IP and the main memory. We will discuss the implementation of concurrency in terms of sharing the IP and the main memory among several processes.

14.2 Memory Allocation

Modern programming languages such as Ada are designed to match a specific memory model shown in Figure 14.1.

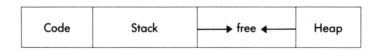

Figure 14.1 Memory model for programming languages

The object code is stored in one segment. The code segment is never modified and can even be stored in *read-only memory (ROM)*. The nested block structure

---

[1] We are ignoring complications like variable length instructions.

means that memory needed by a procedure call can be allocated on a *stack*. When a procedure is called, a block of stack memory called the *activation record* is allocated which contains memory locations for parameters and local variables as well as room to store the *return address* – the address of the instruction after the procedure call. Upon return from a procedure, the IP is loaded with this value. This technique is what allows us to call the same procedure from several locations in a program. Finally, the activation record contains pointers used by the procedure to access variables in global environments. The third area is called the *heap*. Programming languages contain statements for dynamically creating data structures that are then accessed by pointers rather than variable names. This memory is allocated from the heap.

The size of the code area is known at compilation time. The stack grows and contracts dynamically. Its size is not a function of how many procedures exist or how often they are called since upon exit from a procedure space is automatically reclaimed. Instead it is a function of the maximum depth of procedure calls and of the amount of local memory needed by the procedures. If the program contains recursive procedures, the size of the stack cannot be calculated in advance.[2] If not, the maximum stack size can be calculated, though this may impractical in a large program. Heap storage requirements cannot be calculated in advance since dynamic allocation is usually used for data structures like lists and trees whose size depend on the input to the program.

To summarize:

- Code size is fixed at compilation.

- Stack size can often be estimated before execution. The stack is well behaved: expanding and contracting at one end with no wasted space.

- Heap size is unpredictable. The heap is not well behaved because allocation and de-allocation of variable-sized data areas can occur at any time and at any place within the heap.

What are the implications for concurrency?

- The code areas of the processes are independent and can simply be concatenated together. In fact, code sharing is possible; several processes can use the same object code for a procedure called by any of them.

- The stack contains information particular to each process. The state of the process is defined by its IP (and other registers) and the contents of its memory locations such as procedure variables, parameters, etc. Thus each process will need to have its own stack.

- The heap can be shared since once a data area is allocated it is just like any other memory location and each process will access the locations it was allocated. However, since allocation does modify the heap which is global to all processes, mutual exclusion must be imposed to ensure its consistency.

---

[2] A similar problem exists if local variables can have their size determined at run-time as allowed in Ada but not in Pascal.

As shown in Figure 14.1, since the stack grows in only one direction, the heap is allocated at the other end of the memory and allowed to grow in the opposite direction. This gives some flexibility in that the same locations can be used by one area and later on by the other. If the two areas meet, then there is actually no more memory to allocate. To implement concurrency, it is not enough to set the bottom of the stack and hope that it does not meet the heap. A stack must be allocated to each process so we must provide the run-time system with an estimate of the stack size of each process (Figure 14.2). This data structure is called a *cactus stack* since a stack is linked to the stack of the process which allocated it.

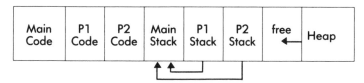

Figure 14.2 Stack allocation for concurrency

A good compiler would make a reasonable first guess for the stack size, but this may not be accurate. In any case, there is a possibility that one process may run out of stack space even when there is free memory. One possibility is to re-arrange the stack allocation at run-time, though this may be difficult on some architectures since the activation records contain pointers to memory locations within the stack. In any case, re-arranging the stacks can time consuming and is not appropriate for real-time systems.

A minor variation on the cactus stack is to allocate the stacks directly from the heap rather than maintaining a separate area for the stacks. This has the advantage that only a single allocation mechanism is needed and the disadvantage that if stack re-arrangement is attempted, it has to be integrated with the heap storage reclamation system.

Heap allocation also poses special problems in concurrent programs. In a sequential system, a request for more memory than is currently available is considered an error. In a concurrent system, it might be reasonable to suspend the requesting process in the hope that another process will eventually free enough memory for the suspended process to proceed. Alternatively, an indication could be returned to the requesting process. In a critical system, the process can be designed to exhibit degraded behavior or to raise an alarm, either of which is preferable to aborting the program.

Heap allocation strategies usually maintain lists of free and allocated memory blocks. Both allocation and release of memory can be time consuming or unpredictable because the time depends on the length of the lists. Concurrent programs with time constraints may need special algorithms which limit the unpredictability of the response time of memory allocation algorithms. In extreme cases, they may have to forego dynamic allocation.

Garbage collection is the term given to reclamation of heap storage that is no longer accessible. It is an alternative to requiring the programmer to explicitly free unused memory. Garbage collection is an essential part of advanced languages like Prolog and LISP. Its main drawback is that classical algorithms require that all computation must be suspended for a long time at unpredictable intervals for the collector to work. Concurrent algorithms exist which allow garbage collection to be done by a separate process, spreading out the overhead throughout the computation. On a multi-processor, a separate processor can be allocated to garbage collection, almost eliminating the overhead on the real-time computation.

14.3   Process Control Blocks

The previous section described the static arrangement of memory required to support concurrency. We still need to dynamically share the (single) processor among the various processes. Since each process will be interrupted or blocked during its execution we need to store data concerning the state of the process. At the very least, the IP must be saved. For each process, we define a data structure called the *process control block* (PCB) used to store the state of the process.

At any instant, at most one process will be executing on the processor. The status of this process is *running*. There may be contention for the processor, that is there may be other processes that are *ready* to execute. The PCBs of these processes are linked together in the *ready queue* (Figure 14.3). Whenever it becomes necessary to change the process that is allocated to the processor, an operating system routine called the *scheduler* takes one process from the ready queue and sets the IP from the PCB. The current IP first saved in the PCB of the executing process which is linked into a queue. This processing is called *context switching* and is the principal overhead of concurrent programming on a single processor.

Figure 14.3 Process control blocks

Since the executing process is the one executing on the processor, what can cause it to invoke the scheduler to change the executing process? In the simplest common-memory models (load-and-store or test-and-set), the answer is nothing. Scheduling must be artificially invoked by a hardware timer which interrupts the processor periodically. This time-slicing cuts up the available processing time into fixed-length intervals which can then be allocated to the processes by the scheduler.

In the case of blocking primitives like semaphores, monitors and rendezvous, a process will explicitly indicate its willingness to relinquish the computer. While time-slicing is no longer required, it is usually implemented if for no other reason then to allow the system to interrupt a process in an infinite loop. For each blocking primitive there will be a logically separate queue (Figure 14.4):

- For each semaphore.
- For each monitor and for each condition variable.
- For each entry and for delayed processes in Ada.

Signaling primitives will check the appropriate queue and move a PCB to the ready queue. To separate different aspects of the system into different software modules, the signaling primitive will not attempt to schedule the awakened process but will call the regular scheduler on the updated ready queue. The immediate resumption requirement of the monitor primitive can be implemented by inserting the PCB into the ready queue at the place where the scheduler is known to choose the next process.

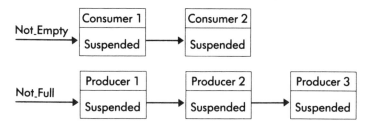

Figure 14.4 Queues for blocking primitives

14.4 Priorities

Scheduling of processes is done by assigning a number to each process called its *priority*. The priorities may be statically assigned at compilation time as in Ada, or they be computed dynamically during run time. Chapter 16 discusses priority allocation strategies.

If the ready queue is ordered in decreasing priority, the next process to run is just the process at the head of the queue. Insertion of a ready process requires the scheduler to search the queue. The insertion will be facilitated if a doubly-linked list is used (Figure 14.5).

If there are a large number of processes and a small number of priority values an alternative data structure is one that maintains an array of queues of PCBs, one queue for each priority value (Figure 14.6). Insertion is simplified since no search is required – the process is simply appended to the tail of the queue for its priority (implicitly breaking ties of equal priority processes on the basis of time of arrival). Selecting the next process to run requires a search for a non-empty queue. If the search is done in order of decreasing priority, high priority processes will be found immediately and only low priority processes will incur significant overhead which is a reasonable design objective.

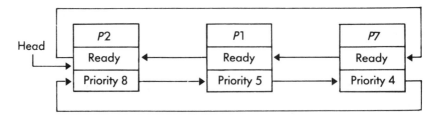

Figure 14.5 Doubly-linked list ordered by priority

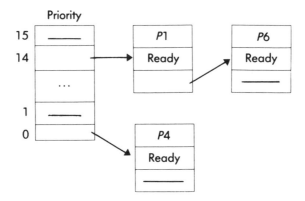

Figure 14.6 Array of queues

Similar techniques are used on the blocking queues. To implement a delay queue, the PCBs are constructed in order of increasing time until wake-up. At every timer update, processes whose wake-up time have passed are moved from the delay queue to the ready queue. We can see how a `delay` statement in Ada does not ensure that a process will actually be run within the time specified in the `delay`. *After* the period of time has elapsed, the process will be moved to the ready queue and then it must compete according to priority with other processes.

The FIFO queues required by blocked queue semaphores, monitor condition variables and Ada `accept` statements are implemented by ordering the PCBs in increasing time-of-arrival. In Figure 14.5, circular lists are used where the tail of the list is linked to the head. Insertion at the tail can now be done in constant time.

14.5 The Ada Rendezvous

Implementation of the rendezvous is more complex because a task may have several entries and it may conditionally wait on those entries (Figure 14.7). Let us consider first a simple `accept` statement and then the `select` statement. When

```
loop
  accept Init do ... ;
  select
    when Guard_1 => accept E1(...) do ... ;
  or
    when Guard_2 => accept E2(...) do ... ;
  or
    when Guard_3 => accept E3(...) do ... ;
  end select;
end loop;
```

Figure 14.7 A typical Ada task

an entry is called and the accepting task is not yet ready to accept, the calling task must be suspended. Two obvious choices for data structures are (Figure 14.8):

- Maintain a single list of PCBs for all calling tasks.
- Maintain a separate list for each entry.

The second alternative is to be preferred unless there are very many entries and very few calls expected. If there are separate lists for each entry, when an `accept` statement is executed one can index directly to the proper list and commence the rendezvous with the first task on the list.

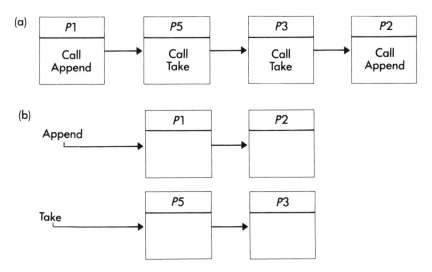

Figure 14.8 Data structures for entry queues

The PCB of the task suspended in the entry queue should have a pointer to a block of memory where the parameters of the call are stored. The accepting task can then copy the parameters, perform the statements of the rendezvous and update the parameters to terminate the rendezvous. Then *both* tasks are inserted into the ready queue and the scheduler is called to find the task with the highest priority.

The other possibility in a rendezvous is that the entry queues are empty and the accepting task must be suspended. The PCB of the accepting task will contain an indication that the task is suspended. The call will cause the accepting task to be awakened and placed on the ready queue.

The `select` statement is more difficult to implement because entry calls must be checked against a set of open alternatives: those `accept` statements with guards that evaluate to true. What data structure should be used to describe this set? Again, the choice is between a list and an array (Figure 14.9). If there are many branches in the `select` statement, few of which are expected to be open, a list will more efficient. If an array is used, every element must be updated with the result of the guard evaluation but it will be easy to locate the element for any particular entry.

This data structure is accessed both by the entry call and by the `select` statement evaluation:

- On entry call, the data structure must be checked to see if the accepting process is waiting on an open alternative for this entry. If an array is used, the check can be done in constant time, otherwise a list must be searched.

- When the `select` statement is evaluated, the data structure is created by the evaluation of the guards. Then the entry queues must be checked to see if there are calls queued for the open alternatives. If an array is used, we must sequence through the elements, checking the entry queue(s) for each open alternatives. If a list is used for the open alternatives, the entry queue(s) are checked for each element of the list. This will be more efficient than an array if there are many closed alternatives.

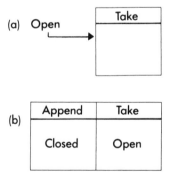

Figure 14.9 Data structures for open alternatives

The other features of the rendezvous are not difficult to implement as extensions of the selective wait:

Else alternative After checking the open alternatives against the entry queue(s), the task does not suspend if a rendezvous is impossible.

Delay alternative The task not only suspends itself, as described above, but also places itself on the delay queue. The processing of the delay queue must be modified so that if this task is awakened, the rendezvous must be canceled. Similarly, if a rendezvous is accomplished during the delay interval, the task must be removed from the delay queue.

Conditional entry call The calling task does not suspend itself on an entry queue if a check of the accepting task shows that it is not suspended awaiting rendezvous or if the alternative for this entry is closed.

Timed entry call As in a conditional entry call except that the calling task suspends itself on the delay queue. As in a selective wait with delay, the delay queue processing and the rendezvous processing must be coordinated.

14.6 Further Reading

Techniques for implementing concurrency are standard and can be found in texts on data structures and operating systems ([Sta80], [Dei85], [PS85]). The special requirements of Ada are described in [BR85]. Algorithms for concurrent garbage collection (called 'on-the-fly' garbage collection in the literature) are presented in [DLM78] and [Ben84].

Chapter 15

Multi-processor Implementation

15.1 Introduction

The implementation of distributed systems is the subject of much experimentation. The essential tradeoff is in the design of the connectivity of the system. Can all processors directly communicate with each other or is the topology more limited? It is convenient to distinguish three families of architectures:

Common memory (Figure 15.1) Even a small amount of common memory enables processors to communicate and synchronize. A larger amount of common memory will hold data needed by all processors. Common-memory architectures are efficient but cannot be expanded to a very large number of processors, both because of the difficulty of constructing the hardware and because of increasing contention for the memory bus. This architecture is common on very-high performance systems that cooperate to solve computationally intensive problems.

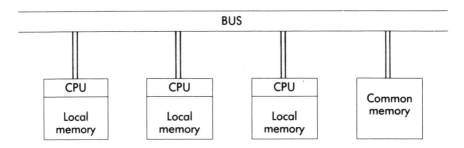

Figure 15.1 Common memory architecture

Networks (Figure 15.2) All processors can still communicate directly as well as broadcast messages to the whole group. The traffic is increased because data structures must be replicated. The hardware scales easily to a relatively large number of processes but increasing contention eventually limits the size of the network. The main use of networks is to connect together independent systems that need to exchange data but do not co-operate on solving problems.

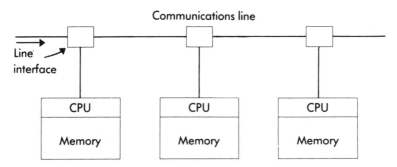

Figure 15.2 Computer network

Point-to-point connectivity (Figure 15.3) Dedicated high-speed communications lines pass data from one processor to another with no contention and no need for addressing. If each processor is connected to only a small number of others, like an array, there is no limit to the size of the system. This architecture is used on high-performance systems that need a very large number of processors. The difficulty is then to construct a program that matches the restrictions of the architecture.

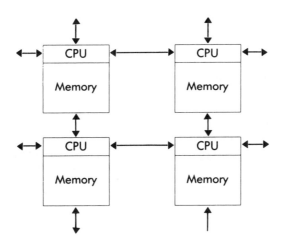

Figure 15.3 Point-to-point architecture

We will describe the transputer system that can deliver very high performance on the restricted occam model and then implementations of Linda on all these architectures. The chapter closes with a discussion of distributed implementation of Ada.

15.2   occam on the Transputer

The transputer is a microprocessor developed by Inmos Corporation to directly support the occam programming model. The IMS 800 transputer (Figure 15.4) contains a fast 32-bit processor, a floating point processor, a small amount (4K bytes) of on-chip memory and four bi-directional high-speed serial communication links. Each directly implements a pair of occam channels, one in each direction.

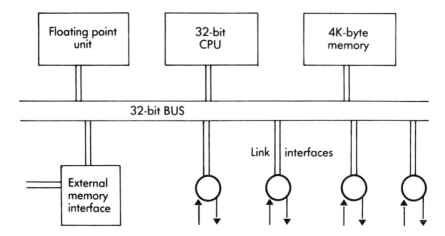

Figure 15.4 IMS 800 transputer architecture

An entire message can be transferred using a single machine instruction. The instruction has three operands: the channel number, the address of the message and the count of the number of bytes in the message. The same instruction is used both for internal channels (between processes that have been allocated on the same transputer) and for external channels (between processes on different transputers). Thus a program that runs on one transputer will run on a multiple transputer system.

The rendezvous semantics of communications require synchronization between input and output. For concreteness, let us assume that one process executes an Output instruction on a channel and then later the other process executes an Input instruction. The execution of the Output instruction depends on the type of channel:

Internal channel The request for communication is noted in a data structure associated with each channel.

External channel The message operands are copied into registers within the link interface.

In both cases, the process is suspended as required by the rendezvous semantics.

Eventually, the process on the other end of the channel reaches the corresponding Input instruction:

Internal channel Checking the channel data structure, it notes that an output request exists and copies the message into its own buffer.

External channel It initializes the registers of its link interface. Now a hardware implemented protocol transfers the message over the channel. The message is transferred byte by byte and each byte is acknowledged through the opposite direction of the link. Note that each link is simultaneously used for data transfer in one direction and acknowledge messages in the other (Figure 15.5).

When message transfer is complete, both processes are released from suspension.

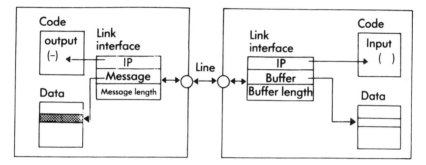

Figure 15.5 Transputer I/O

Remember that occam encourages the creation of a large number of concurrent processes. Scheduling these processes is also implemented by hardware instructions. The transputer maintains two queues of ready processes: high priority and low priority. Normally a process is allowed to run without interruption until it reaches a *descheduling point* which are I/O instructions and termination of processes and loops. Also, high priority processes which become ready because of an external rendezvous occurs will interrupt low priority processes. Otherwise, processes are allowed to execute until they reach a descheduling point. Low priority processes are not run unless the high priority queue is empty. Low priority processes are time-sliced approximately once every 2 milliseconds. This priority model is appropriate if high priority processes are used only to implement short I/O routines.

The advantages of the transputer for high-performance concurrency can be seen by comparing order of magnitude execution times with classical architectures. Channel communication can achieve a rate of about 2 megabytes per second. That means that five 32-bit words can be sent from one transputer to another in 10 microseconds. The hardware scheduler is extremely fast and can do a context switch in one microsecond. Real-time operating systems for classical microcomputers may need 100 microseconds or more to do a context switch in software, and hundreds of microseconds to send a message from one processor to another over a dedicated communications line. Sending a message between large computers over networks can take a millisecond or more when the overhead of the operating system is taken into account.

Clearly, the transputer/occam combination is able to achieve impressive performance in implementing concurrency at the price of restrictions on the allowable hardware and software architecture.

15.3 Implementations of Linda

To implement Linda, we have to implement a global *tuple space* (TS) with insertion and blocking removal of tuples. If there exists common memory on the system, the TS may be stored there. The implementation problem reduces to the classical problem of storing and searching a large data structure. The choice of data structure is dictated by the form of the data. If we have any knowledge that the data are restricted to numbers, are of fixed length, are ordered and so on, we can use this knowledge to choose an optimized data structure. A TS, however, is composed of tuples of arbitrary length, each element of which can be of any type.

With this lack of restriction on the data format, we could store all the tuples in a single linear list. However, searching would be prohibitively expensive. *Hashing* can dramatically improve the search performance by arbitrarily assigning each tuple to one of a large number of very small lists called *bins* (Figure 15.6). A *hashing function* takes the tuple and considering it just as a sequence of bits, computes the number of the bin in which it will be stored. To search for a specific tuple, all we have to do is compute the bin number using the hashing function and search for it in the bin. The hashing function is chosen to be quick to compute and the small bin size ensures that the tuple will be quickly found if it exists.

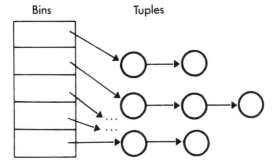

Figure 15.6 Hashing implementation

In Linda, the hashing function is usually computed on the first argument of the tuple only. This leads to a requirement that the first argument of any tuple be an actual value and not a formal parameter.

There exist multi-computer architectures with common memory. However, even on these architectures, it is still more efficient to access local memory than common memory. The recommended programming style in Linda is to use the

TS to store common data but to copy tuples to local memory for computation. Thus in the matrix multiplication example, we stored the rows and columns in the TS, but indexing through the vectors to compute the inner product was done after they were copied into local memory.

Hashing can also be used to implement Linda on an architecture without common memory but with high-speed communications lines like a transputer array or higher level generalizations called *hypercubes* (Figure 15.7). The global TS will be distributed. Each tuple will be stored on one of the processors determined by the result of the hashing function. To locate a tuple, compute the identity of the processor where its bin is stored and send a message requesting the tuple to that processor. With high-speed communications lines this can be efficient.

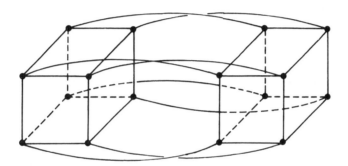

Figure 15.7 Hypercube architecture

Finally, Linda has been implemented on networks where every processor is connected to a single high-speed bus (Figure 15.8). There are two approaches to a network implementation. The TS can be replicated on each processor or it can be distributed among the processors. In the first case, Output broadcasts each tuple. When a processor tries to input or read a tuple, the TS exists locally and the search is efficient. If no matching tuple exists, the process suspends until some incoming tuple matches.

Some mechanism must exist to ensure that the tuple is not removed by two different processors. This can be done by associating each tuple with the processor that created it and requesting permission from this processor before removing the tuple. The 'owning' processor can then ensure that only one processor succeeds in removing the tuple.

The other possibility is to distribute the TS by having each processor locally store the tuples it creates. Now Input and Read must broadcast a request if a matching tuple is not found locally. A receiving processor that matches the request with a local tuple sends it to the requesting processor. It is possible that a processor receives several tuples in answer to its request. In this case, it 'uses' one of them and stores the others. These tuples still exist in the distributed TS even though they may have moved from their original place.

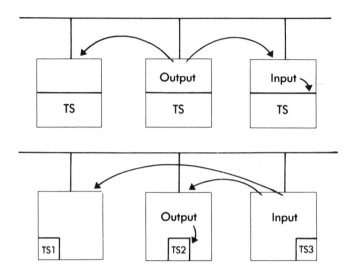

Figure 15.8 Network implementation of tuple space

15.4   Ada on Distributed Systems

It is difficult to implement full Ada on a distributed system. The reason is that the tasking model is integrated into the stack and heap model discussed in the previous chapter on single processor systems.

The first problem is the block structure with its nesting of tasks like ordinary procedures. In Figure 15.9 we see that two tasks can access ordinary global variables as well as global procedures. In a distributed system we have to ask: where are these global data and code located? If they are in one processor, there will be a lot of communication. If they are replicated, we will have problems ensuring consistency. The problem can be complicated if we note that Ada is intended for large systems and the package facility can be used to create a large amount of data and code.

The other problem is the use of dynamic memory allocation. When memory is allocated from a heap, a pointer – an absolute address – is returned. There is no syntactic or semantic limitation in Ada that would prevent two tasks from cooperating on the creation of a list by having each one allocate alternate nodes. If we have one heap on one of the processors, the implementation could be very inefficient. If both processors allocate from their own heaps, how can such a mixed list be implemented?

A related problem is that a pointer can be passed as a parameter in a rendezvous. What does it mean for a task allocated to one processor to receive an absolute address on another?

One solution is to use the concept of *virtual nodes*. During the design of an Ada program, we decide what the maximum number of physically distributed processors will be. These will be called virtual nodes and every component of

```
procedure Main_Program is
  V: array(1..2000) of Integer;

  procedure P(I: in out Integer) is  ... ;

  task T1;
  task body T1 is
  begin
    V(2) := V(3) + 1;
    P(V(2));
  end T1;

  task T2;
  task body T2 is
  begin
    V(2) := V(3) + 2;
    P(V(2));
  end T2;
end Main_Program;
```

Figure 15.9 Block structure in Ada

the program (tasks and packages) will be assigned to some node. Communication between virtual nodes of the program will be limited to parameters that can be easily copied during a rendezvous. Within the virtual node full Ada can be used.

We can always assign more than one virtual node to a single processor, but this design ensures that if nodes are in fact assigned to different processors, they can communicate efficiently over channels. The occam-like restrictions on the program architecture are thus consciously applied by the designer where necessary rather than imposed on all components by the language. Similarly, Linda-like expressibility of common memory is used where needed and not imposed.

This comparison of the three formalisms shows that the designer of a distributed system can choose between expressibility and efficiency and also between a language that imposes (and hence optimizes) one view and a more flexible language that requires more on the part of the designer. Linda and full Ada are very expressive but less efficient than occam in a distributed implementation. Linda and occam impose and optimize a specific primitive while Ada has a more flexible set of primitives.

15.5 Further Reading

The transputer reference manual is [In85]. Implementations of Linda are described in [ACG86]. Virtual nodes in Ada is from [TCN84] which is a study of the use of Ada in distributed environments.

Chapter 16

Real-Time Programming

16.1 Introduction

Real-time programs are programs that must execute within strict constraints on response time. Such programs are used in *embedded computer systems* which have a computer as only one of a set of components that together comprise a large system. Examples are:

- Aircraft and spacecraft flight control systems.
- Industrial plant controllers.
- Medical monitors.
- Communications networks.

The special difficulty in designing real-time systems is in the strict requirement to meet processing deadlines and not in the actual speed of processing. Here are two examples of challenging, complex computer systems which are not real-time:

- Simulation of weather patterns to develop a forecast. This requires the use of powerful supercomputers but it is not a critical failure if the answers are received ten minutes late.

- An airline reservation system must process hundreds or thousands of transactions continuously. A large network of computers, data bases and communications lines is needed to implement the system. The response time requirement for such a system can be expressed statistically. For example: 95 percent of the transactions completed within 5 seconds and 99 percent within 15 seconds.

We do not want to imply that these systems should not be designed to meet deadlines all the time. However, if that would require extremely expensive or unreliable implementation techniques, there is some flexibility in satisfying response time requirements.

A real-time system need not be complex or high-performance. Checking radioactivity levels in a nuclear power plant or pulse rate on a patient may require only the simplest processing that can be done by any micro-computer. However, delay in decreasing plant power or sounding an alarm can be literally fatal. Another problem, common in flight control systems, is that absolute time may be a parameter in the computation. If an algorithm is designed to sample the aircraft state and control its flight every 50 milliseconds, it must be executed at that rate, not faster and not slower (within some tolerance). In real-time systems, neither deadline slippage nor statistical performance is acceptable.

Of course, even in real-time systems, there will be non-real-time tasks such as logging messages and background testing of the hardware. However, when there are real-time tasks, this affects the design of the system and special techniques are needed. The techniques are not as well developed as concurrent programming techniques that ignore absolute time. Nevertheless, the best approach to real-time systems seems to be the careful application of concurrent programming techniques, modified or restricted as needed to construct a successful program.

16.2   Synchronous and Asynchronous Systems

There are two approaches to the implementation of real-time systems: synchronous clock-driven or asynchronous interrupt-driven. In a synchronous system, a hardware clock is used to divide the available processor time into intervals called *frames* (Figure 16.1). The program must then be divided into segments so that every segment can be completed *in the worst case* during a single frame. A scheduling table is constructed which assigns the segments to frames so that all the segments in a frame are completed by the end of the frame. When the clock signals the beginning of the frame, the scheduler of the underlying system calls the various segments as described in the table. If a computation is too long to fit in one frame, it must be artificially split into smaller segments that can be individually scheduled.

Figure 16.2 shows an Ada task executing as a synchronous scheduler. Each frame commences by sampling an input. The computation is divided into even and odd cycles. Following the computation, control signals are sent to the output

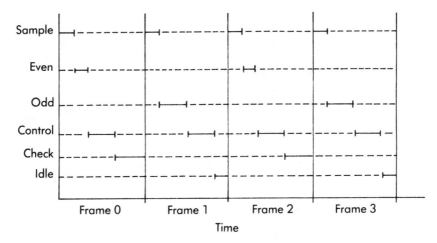

Figure 16.1 Synchronous systems

```
task body Synchronous is
  Frame: Integer range 0..3 := 0;
begin
  loop
    accept Clock_Interrupt;   -- No accept body
    case Frame is
      when 0 => Sample;
                Compute_Even;
                Control_Device;
                Check_Input_Failure;
      when 1 => Sample;
                Compute_Odd;
                Control_Device;
      when 2 => Sample;
                Compute_Even;
                Control_Device;
                Check_Output_Failure;
      when 3 => Sample;
                Compute_Odd;
                Control_Device;
    end case;
    Frame := (Frame+1) mod 4;
  end loop;
end Synchronous;
```

Figure 16.2 Synchronous scheduler

devices. The computation on the even cycles is shorter than on the odd cycles so in those frames we also check for hardware failures. The assignment of segments to frames is shown in Figure 16.1.

An asynchronous system does not attempt to divide the computation into segments. Instead, each segment executes to completion and then the scheduler is called to find the next task to execute. This is the Ada model where the tasks themselves execute asynchronously and the rendezvous exists if it is necessary to synchronize them. Two extensions to this model need to be made in order to write real-time software in an asynchronous system. The various tasks must be given priority so that we can be assured that critical tasks like Sample and Control are always executed even at the expense of background tasks like Check_Input_Failure.

In addition, *pre-emptive scheduling* must be implemented to ensure that a high-priority task can execute as soon as it becomes ready, even if that means suspending the execution of a task of lower priority (Figure 16.3). Ada requires that pre-emptive scheduling be implemented. A higher priority task can become ready upon expiration of a delay or if an interrupt occurs. Closely related to pre-emptive scheduling is *time-slicing* which divides available processor time among several tasks of equal priority. This is implemented by a hardware timer which interrupts processing periodically to allow the scheduler to search for another task to execute. The Ada standard does not require an implementation to implement time-slicing, though most do so.

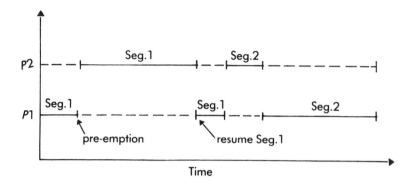

Figure 16.3 Asynchronous systems

The choice between the two types of system hinges on the price one is willing to pay for guaranteed response time. Synchronous systems absolutely guarantee that the tasks will be executed at a rate determined by the timer and the scheduling table provided that there is no overflow of the computation during a frame. However, the scheduling table must be constructed using worst-case timings of each task. If, on the average, the tasks execute faster there is no way to use the wasted processor time. In addition, the fixed size frames will cause fragmentation overhead because segments may not fit in the leftover space in a frame. For example, if every segment is at least 15 milliseconds long, when a 50 millisecond frame has segments totaling more than 35 milliseconds assigned, the rest of the time is wasted. These problems are similar to those experienced in paged virtual memory operating systems. The problems here are more serious because processor time in a real-time system is more significant than memory utilization in a multi-programming computer system.

In addition, since the length of the frames is fixed, segments will be run at integral multiples of the frame length, regardless of the actual requirements. With 50 millisecond frames, a segment that need only run every 75 milliseconds must be run at the higher rate of 50 milliseconds, wasting processor time.

In an asynchronous system, no processor time is ever wasted. As long as there are tasks on the ready queue, some process will always be executing and we can achieve 100 percent utilization. Overall, the computations will be completed faster. However, it is difficult to ensure that any particular computation will be executed within any particular deadline. Obviously, the highest priority task can pre-empt any running task and execute immediately. As we descend in priority, a task will be executed within a time interval that is determined by the actual execution times of the higher-priority tasks. In practice, it may not be possible to compute this time interval.

There is another reason to prefer asynchronous systems. The segmentation of the computation and the construction of the scheduling tables is extremely difficult and error-prone. Moreover, a change in system requirements or in the hardware will invalidate the tables and require their reconstruction. Asynchronous systems by nature dynamically re-adjust themselves to the demand from the various processes.

It seems that the best solution is to used a mixed system. Use a synchronous computation for a few truly time-critical tasks and asynchronous tasks in the background that execute in the available time (Figure 16.4).

```
task body Synchronous is
  Frame: Integer range 0..1 := 0;
begin
  loop
    accept Clock_Interrupt;   -- No accept body
    case Frame is
      when 0 => Sample;
                Compute_Even;
                Control_Device;
      when 1 => Sample;
                Compute_Odd;
                Control_Device;
    end case;
    Frame := (Frame+1) mod 2;
  end loop;
end Synchronous;

task body Check_Input_Failure is ... ;

task body Check_Output_Failure is ... ;
```

Figure 16.4 Mixed system

16.3   Interrupts and Polling

The choice between synchronous and asynchronous designs for a real-time system extends to I/O drivers within the system. In the example of a synchronous system, the procedure Sample will read the channels or registers connected to the input devices and similarly for Control_Device. I/O that is done periodically at the initiative of the program is called *polling*. For polling to work, an input device must be able to maintain its value on the channel until it is sampled by the processor. Other problems can occur if I/O devices are not adapted to polling. The optimal rate of I/O may not be a multiple of frame duration or the I/O device may not respond immediately to a command. However, polling does not introduce any difficulty in the programming itself since I/O is done sequentially within the frame like any other computation.

Just as synchronous systems pay a high price in efficiency to obtain predictability, polling can be extremely inefficient so most I/O devices work on asynchronous *interrupts*. Conceptually, the I/O operation is regarded as an asynchronous process of higher priority than the computational processes. When an I/O device is ready it is scheduled pre-emptively.

The implementation of interrupts is not the same as that of software processes. Associated with each interrupt is a process called the *interrupt handler*. The address of an interrupt handler is stored in a fixed memory location called the *interrupt vector* (Figure 16.5). An interrupt is initiated by an I/O device. This causes the interrupt handler to be scheduled, pre-empting whatever software process happens to be running. The scheduling is done by the hardware and not by the software scheduler. A partial context switch is done; at the very minimum, the IP of the running process must be stored so that it can be restored upon completion of the interrupt. Unlike software processes, interrupt handlers should terminate and should be as short as possible since they run at the highest priority.

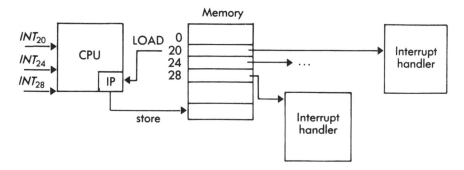

Figure 16.5 Interrupts

The interrupt mechanism is so useful that it is also used by the processor itself to indicate faults like division by zero. In addition, many computers contain instructions available to the programmer that are implemented by interrupts:

Trap Used to catch instructions that have not been implemented in hardware. The interrupt handler is a software emulation of the instruction.

Breakpoint Used by the debugger to replace an ordinary instruction. The interrupt handler is the debugger software which allows the programmer to query the status of the computation.

Supervisor calls Interrupts are used rather than procedure calls to ensure that the operating system runs at higher priority than ordinary processes.

Despite the differing implementation, interrupt handlers should be regarded as ordinary asynchronous processes for which concurrent programming techniques of synchronization and communication are applicable.

16.4 Interrupt Handlers and Software Processes

Suppose we have a set of software processes running at priorities 1–10. Conceptually, an interrupt occurs with a higher priority, say 20, so that it pre-empts any software process. What priority should be given to the interrupt handler process? The simplest decision is to run the interrupt handler at an even higher priority, say 30, so that it is uninterruptible. This simplifies the programming of device drivers, debuggers, operating systems, etc. since they have become critical sections running under mutual exclusion from all other critical sections.

While interrupt handlers are critical sections, the problem remains of how do we synchronize and communicate with the software processes? In Figure 16.6 we see that even though the variable N is incremented under mutual exclusion in the interrupt handler, no such mutual exclusion exists in the software process.

```
N: Integer := 0;

task body Interrupt_Handler is
begin
  N := N + 1;
end Interrupt_Handler;

task body Software_Process is
begin
  loop
    ...
    N := N + 1;
    ...
    N := N + 1;
    ...
  end loop;
end Software_Process;
```

Figure 16.6 Synchronization with interrupt handlers

There are two solutions to this problem:

1. Transfer all critical sections from the software processes to software-invoked interrupt handlers.

2. Use non-blocking producer–consumer schemes to transfer data to and from the interrupt handlers.

The first solution returns us to the realm of concurrent programming, but the overhead may be unacceptable for real-time programs. In fact, it is possible to implement concurrent programming by decomposing all the software into interrupt handlers! There is no operating system as such and every statement can assume mutual exclusion if the handlers themselves are not interrupted. This design would be appropriate in a system that is demand-driven by I/O device requests, each of which requires relatively little processing.

The second solution is more often used in real-time systems. For concreteness, let us assume that an interrupt handler is reading data from an input device and passing it to a computational process. The producer–consumer solutions that we programmed require the producer to suspend itself when the buffer is full and similarly for the consumer when the buffer is empty. Suspending the consuming computational process is no problem, but we do not want to suspend the high-priority interrupt handler producer. Obviously, the buffer should be designed so that overflow is rare, but we still have to decide what to do if it does occur. There are two choices:

Lost data New data are discarded if the buffer is full.

Fresh data New data overwrite 'stale' data if the buffer is full.

Figure 16.7 shows the difference in programming the two designs.

```
-- Lost data
  if Count = N then
    null;
  else
    B(In_Ptr) := Value;
    Count := Count + 1;
    In_Ptr := (In_Ptr+1) mod N;
  end if;

-- Fresh data
  if Count = N then
    Out_Ptr := (Out_Ptr + 1) mod N;
  else
    Count := Count + 1;
  end if;
  B(In_Ptr) := Value;
  In_Ptr := (In_Ptr+1) mod N;
```

Figure 16.7 Non-blocking producers

The lost data option can be chosen when sequential processing of the data is important and when retry can be attempted. In a communications system, it is important to deliver a complete message and occasional retransmission of lost data will not significantly degrade the performance of the system. On the other hand, the fresh data option is chosen in control systems which try to predict or control future behavior based on past samples. It is less important to know where the aircraft was half a second ago or what the patient's pulse rate was ten seconds ago than it is to know the value of those signals *now*.

16.5 Nested Interrupts

Computer hardware usually provides the ability to assign interrupts to a set of *levels*. Through software commands, it is possible to dynamically change the set of levels from which interrupts will be accepted. The previous section considered the simple case where all levels are enabled except when an interrupt handler is executing in which case all levels are disabled. The other extreme would be to leave all levels enabled. This is equivalent to pre-emptive scheduling with no priority and has little to recommend it.

One design which is commonly used is to consider the levels as priorities and enable higher priority interrupts during the execution of an interrupt handler. This is called *nested interrupts* because higher priority interrupt handlers are executed as is they were nested local procedures (Figure 16.8). This design is attractive because each handler can assume that is it executed as a critical section with respect to lower priority interrupt handlers as well as the software processes. Furthermore, since interrupts of the same priority are disabled, an interrupt handler does not have run under mutual exclusion with 'itself'. For example, if we use one of the buffering schemes described earlier to communicate with a software process, an interrupt handler can safely execute instructions like In_Ptr := In_Ptr+1 without invoking a synchronization primitive.

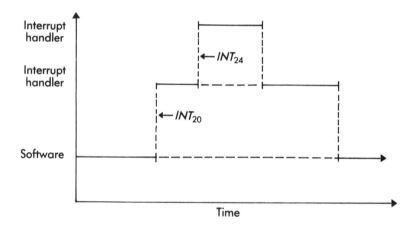

Figure 16.8 Nested interrupts

16.6   Scheduling Algorithms for Real-Time

How should priorities be assigned to processes in a real-time system? In this section we present (without proofs) two results on scheduling algorithms.

Assume that we are given a set of processes Pi each of which is characterized by a repetition interval Int_i and an execution duration Ex_i. That is, every Int_i seconds, process Pi requires Ex_i seconds of processor time. A *priority assignment* is an assignment of numbers Pri_i to the processes. The processes are scheduled by a pre-emptive scheduler which interrupts a running process if a higher priority process becomes ready.

The *response time* of a request to execute a process is the time between the request and the completion of the process.[1] A scheduler overflows if a process must execute another cycle before the previous one has been completed. A priority

---

[1] Here we are using process to mean one execution of a cycle of the process.

assignment is *feasible* if a pre-emptive scheduler will execute all processes without overflow.

For example, let $Int_1 = 2$, $Int_2 = 5$, $Ex_1 = 1$ and $Ex_2 = 2$. Assigning priorities such that $Pri_1 > Pri_2$ is feasible. In Figure 16.9(a), P1 completes its execution during the first second of the first two-second interval, leaving an an additional second for P2. At the end of two seconds, P1 pre-empts P2 for its next interval, relinquishing the processor again after one second. This shows that the assignment is feasible since P2 has received $Ex_2 = 2$ seconds within $Int_2 = 5$ seconds.

Conversely, if $Pri_2 > Pri_1$, P1 cannot pre-empt P2 which will proceed to execute for two seconds before relinquishing the processor (Figure 16.9(b)). Thus an $Int_1 = 2$ interval has expired without P1 receiving $Ex_1 = 1$ seconds of processing time and the assignment is not feasible.

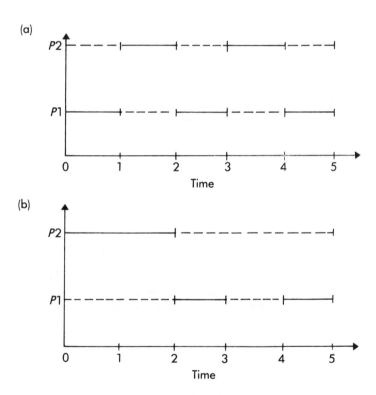

Figure 16.9 Feasible priority assignments

Theorem 16.6.1 *The longest possible response time for a process occurs when it is requested at the same time as all higher priority processes.*

This means that in checking a priority assignment for feasibility, it is sufficient to consider a scenario where all processes are in phase and request service at the same time. This was done in Figure 16.9 to show that only one of the two possible priority assignments is feasible.

The *rate monotonic scheduling algorithm* (RMSA) assigns priorities to processes in decreasing order of the intervals between requests. That is, the faster a process needs to be executed, the higher its priority, regardless of the duration of the process or the 'importance' of the process. It is possible to prove the following surprising result:

Theorem 16.6.2 *RMSA is optimal: if there exists a feasible priority assignment for a set of processes then RMSA is also feasible.*

Despite the simplicity of the RMSA, there are two problems that may limit its applicability:

- Processor time can be wasted as shown in Figure 16.10. Here $Ex_i = 1$, $Int_1 = 3$, $Int_2 = 4$, and $Int_3 = 5$. The process requests are shown beneath the axis and the processor allocations above. It can be seen that there is unused processor time that cannot be used by other processes scheduled by the algorithm.

- The algorithm is based on a model of fixed repetition rates and fixed execution durations. In practice, this means always using the maximum rate and maximum execution time which causes under-utilization of the time frames.

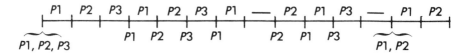

Figure 16.10 Rate monotonic scheduling algorithm

A *deadline* is the time of the next request for a process. The *deadline driven scheduling algorithm* (DDSA) dynamically assigns priorities such that the process with the closest deadline receives the highest priority. This algorithm can fully utilize the processor.

Theorem 16.6.3 *DDSA is feasible if and only if:*

$$\sum_i \frac{Ex_i}{Int_i} \leq 1$$

For the example above, $\frac{1}{3} + \frac{1}{4} + \frac{1}{5} \simeq 0.78$, so it is feasible. In fact, the DDSA would still be feasible if P3 needed 2 seconds to execute because $\frac{1}{3} + \frac{1}{4} + \frac{2}{5} \simeq 0.98$. However, if P1 needed 2 seconds, it would not be feasible: $\frac{2}{3} + \frac{1}{4} + \frac{1}{5} \simeq 1.12$.

DDSA is not always immediately applicable because hardware processes like interrupt routines may have fixed priorities. In addition, it may impose a serious overhead on the real-time scheduler.

16.7 Priority Inversion in Ada

It is not possible to implement rate monotonic scheduling in Ada because of a problem known as *priority inversion*. This occurs because the rendezvous is executed at the higher of the two priorities rather than executing it at the priority of the calling task. In addition, Ada priorities are not considered when choosing among calling tasks queued at an entry (FIFO scheduling is used instead), nor in the choice of alternative in a select statement (the choice is non-deterministic regardless of the priorities of the queued calling tasks).

Suppose task High is executing at priority 8, task Medium at priority 7 and task Low at priority 6. They may all require the services of task Server. What priority should be given to Server? Suppose it is given priority 10, and suppose that Server is engaged in a rendezvous with Low. If High suddenly becomes ready to execute, it ought to be able to pre-empt Server which is doing work for Low. But this is impossible because the rendezvous is executing at priority 10. A priority inversion has occurred between Low and High.

Now let us assume that Server is given priority 5 and is engaged in a rendezvous with Low. Let High and Medium become ready for execution and let High call Server. Since rendezvous execute under mutual exclusion, it is reasonable to assume that High should wait for the conclusion of the rendezvous with Low. Then High should be scheduled in preference to Medium. But upon the conclusion of the rendezvous, Server must issue another select or accept before it can engage in another rendezvous. In the competition between Server at priority 5 and Medium at 6, Medium will win, even though Server should be working for High. A priority inversion has occurred between Medium and High.

16.8 Further Reading

[Mac80] discussed real-time systems in the context of Ada. The real-time scheduling algorithms are from [LL73]. Priority inversion in Ada is from [CS87] and an alternative priority strategy for Ada is suggested in [GS84]. Algorithms for real-time memory allocation are given in [For88].

Appendix A

Ada Overview

A.1 Introduction

This appendix is intended to give an overview of the part of the Ada programming language used in this book. It assumes that the reader is experienced in a high-level programming language, preferably Pascal since Ada is built upon its principles.

Lexically, Ada is written in ASCII characters. It is free-form, meaning that punctuation marks rather than format on the page are used to indicate grammatical units. Identifiers are arbitrary length sequences of letters, numbers and underscores beginning with a letter. Upper and lower case letters are not distinguished. Certain identifiers like procedure, if, loop, end are reserved and may not be used for other purposes. Any Ada book will contain a list of the reserved words. A comment starts with a pair of minus-signs and continues until the end of the line.

An Ada program is a procedure which contains a declarative part followed by a sequence of executable statements (Figure A.1). Every variable and every

```
procedure Main_Program is
  G: Integer := 0;  -- Global variable
                    -- with initial value
  procedure Inner(P: in Integer) is
    L: Integer;  -- Local variable
  begin
    L := P + 1;
    G := L + G; -- Global variable accessible
  end Inner;

begin
  G := G * 5;   -- Sequence of statements
  Inner(7);     -- including procedure call
  G := G + 1;
end Main_Program;
```

Figure A.1 Ada program structure

local procedure must be declared before it is used. An initial value may be given for a variable. Procedure parameters must be declared and the procedure calls must have the correct number and type of parameters. A procedure nested within another can access the declarations in the enclosing scope. Procedure parameters have a *mode* associated with them: `in`, `out`, `in out`. `in` parameters may only be read within the procedure, `out` parameters may only be written and `in out` parameters may be both read and written. In the absence of an explicit mode, `in` is assumed. All parameters of a function must be `in` parameters. An explicit `return` statement is used to terminate the execution of the function and return the computed result:

```
function Square(I: in Integer) return Integer is
begin
  return I * I;
end Square;
```

A.2   Types and Statements

Ada contains predefined types: `Integer`, `Float`, `Character`, `Boolean`. The boolean literals are `False`, `True` and the character literals are ASCII characters in single quotes: `'a'`, `'X'`. The type `String` is also predefined; its values are character sequences within double quotes: `"Good morning"`. The usual arithmetic operations are defined on integer and floating point values.

Statements are terminated by semicolons. They include assignment statements and control statements: `if`, `loop`, `case`, `return`. `elsif` can be used to program additional branches within an `if then else` statement:

```
if A > B then
  C := A;
elsif A < B then
  C := B;
else
  C := 0;
end if;
```

A `loop` statement can be written with no conditional clause in which case it indicates an infinite loop. It can also be controlled by a `for` clause or a `while` clause and in addition, `exit` statements can terminate a loop at any point within its sequence of statements:

```
for I in 1..10 loop
  A(I) := 0;
end loop;
while X > 0 loop
  X := X / 2;
end loop;
loop
  X := X / 2;
  exit when X <= 0;
end loop;
```

The last example shows how an **exit** statement can simulate a Pascal **repeat** statement. We use **exit** extensively in the examples because we are usually interested in waiting for something to occur and this gives a positive statement of the condition for leaving the loop.

Ada provides an extensive facility for creating user defined types:

Enumerations

```
type States is (Off, Run, Start);
```

Arrays

```
type Arr is array(1..100) of Integer;
```

Records

```
type Rec is
  record
    Field1: Integer;
    Field2: Boolean;
  end record;
```

Pointers

```
type Rec_Pointer is access Rec;
```

Tasks See Chapter 8.

Arr is declared above as a constrained array type, which means that its indices are constrained at compilation type and all arrays of this type range over the same indices. *Aggregates* denote values that are entire arrays or records. We use them to initialize arrays:

```
A: array(1..100) of Integer := (others => 0);
```

It is also possible to declare an unconstrained array type and then supply the constraint when the array variable is declared. In particular, strings are implemented this way. To declare a string variable, the index bounds must be given:

```
A1: Arr;            -- A1 has 100 elements
A2: Arr;            --   so does A2

S1: String(1..80);  -- S1 has 80 elements
S2: String(1..40);  -- S2 has 40 elements
S3: String;         -- Invalid.
```

Attributes are functions that are used to access predefined characteristics. For example, States'First and States'Last evaluate to Off and Start, respectively. If the declaration of States is modified, these attributes will evaluate to the new first and last values of the type. There is a rich set of attributes in Ada. Some of the most useful are those defined on arrays: First, Last, Length and **Range**. Using attributes makes it possible to write programs that need not be modified if a declaration is changed.

```
S: String(1..80);
if S'Length < 50 then      -- fewer than 50 elements in S
  S(S'Last) := S(S'First); -- store first element last
```

```
    end if;
    for I in S'Range loop     -- loop for all elements in S
      S(I) := '*';
    end loop;
```

One feature that we will occasionally use is the addition of a *range constraint* to integer variables. This clearly documents the values that such a variable can have. If an attempt is made to assign a value outside the range, the Ada system will detect the fault.

```
    N: Integer range 0..1 := 0;
```

A.3   Packages

The language described so far is just a variant of Pascal. Along with tasking, the package facility is the main distinguishing mark of Ada. Standard Pascal does not contain any structure larger than the procedure except an entire program. Most Pascal compilers do supply a module structure, but this is not done in any uniform way.

A *package* in Ada is a set of data and procedure declarations that can be compiled, placed in a library and later accessed by other packages or by the main program. For example, the standard Ada library contains a package called Text_IO which contains procedures to read and write from a terminal. The program can access the entities in a package by placing a *context clause* before the program:

```
    with Text_IO;
    procedure Main_Program is
    begin
      Text_IO.Put_Line("Good morning");
    end Main_Program;
```

The Text_IO package contains a procedure called Put_Line which takes a parameter of type String, prints the parameter on the terminal followed by the control sequence for end-of-line. The dotted notation is used to access the procedure within the package that is mentioned in the with clause just as if it were a field within a record.

Since we often want to access many of the entities within a package, the context clause can include a use clause which allows us to omit the name of the package. However, if this results in any ambiguity, the full dotted notation must be used.

```
    with Text_IO; use Text_IO;
    procedure Main_Program is
    begin
      Put_Line("Good Morning");
    end Main_Program;
```

Packages are used to decompose large systems into modules. The decomposition itself does not help if we still have to read the entire program to understand what is going on. Packages are written in two parts to separate out the *interface* to the entities in the package from the *implementation*. The users need only see the interface to the package and the implementation can be changed without affecting them. The interface part is called the package *specification* and consists of data declarations and procedure declarations only. The implementation part is called the package *body* and consists of the procedure bodies that implement the procedures that appear in the specification as well as additional data declarations and procedures (Figure A.2).

```
package Geometry is     -- Specification
  function Circle_Area(Radius: in  Float) return Float;
  function Square_Area(Side:   in  Float) return Float;
end Geometry;

package body Geometry is
  PI: Float := 3.14159;    -- Internal data
  function Square(X: in Float) return Float is
  begin                    -- Internal procedure
    return X * X;
  end Square;

  function Circle_Area(Radius: in  Float) return Float is
  begin
    return PI * Square(Radius);
  end Circle_Area;
  function Square_Area(Side:   in  Float) return Float is
  begin
    return Square(Side);
  end Square_Area;

end Geometry;
```

Figure A.2 Package specification and body

In this book, we typically demonstrate concurrent programming primitives on small examples that can be written in a single program. The package facility is used to provide simulations of the various primitives that can be hidden from the reader. For example, the semaphore package specification provides a semaphore type and specifications of the Wait and Signal primitives. Their implementation in Ada is hidden in the package body which would be of interest only to Ada programmers.

Both the package specification and the package body are *compilation units* which can be separately compiled and saved in a library. Tasks are not compilation units; they must be textually included within another unit, usually a package or the main program. However, it is possible to separately compile a procedure, package or task body as shown in Figure A.3. The body is replaced by the word **separate**. This *subunit* can then be placed in a file and separately compiled where a clause identifies the parent unit. The use of **separate** is transparent to the programmer. Visibility within the subunit is the same as if it were textually included in the parent unit. However, any change in the parent unit will require recompilation of the subunit.

```
                procedure Main is
                  task Buffer is
                    entry Append(I: in  Integer);
                    entry Take  (I: out Integer);
                  end Buffer;

                  task Producer;
                  task Consumer;

                  task body Buffer   is separate;
                  task body Producer is separate;
                  task body Consumer is separate;
                begin
                  ...
                end Main;

                separate(Main)
                task body Buffer is ... ;

                separate(Main)
                task body Producer is ...;

                separate(Main)
                task body Consumer is ...;
```

Figure A.3 Separate compilation of subunits

To summarize, Ada has:

- Pascal-like structured control statements.

- Pascal-like block structure of procedures.

- The package facility for modularization.

- Built-in concurrent programming (tasks).

Additional aspects of Ada not used in this book are:

- User defined types that significantly extend the Pascal types.

- User processing of errors called **exceptions**.

- Representation clauses that map programs to hardware.

A.4 Further Reading

The reference manual for Ada is [DOD83]. There are many textbooks on Ada: [Bar89] and [Coh88] are written for experienced programmers who wish to learn Ada, while [WWF87] is appropriate for beginners. [Boo83] is an introduction to designing large systems in Ada, specifically by using packages to implement object-oriented programming.

Appendix B

Concurrent Programs in Ada

B.1   Introduction

Most of the examples shown in this book can be run on Ada systems. The purpose of this appendix is to describe the additional work that must be done to turn the program fragments into executable programs.

Since concurrent programs may not terminate, we must find some means of observing their behavior. One way is to insert print statements into the tasks and the other is to use a good debugger to follow the state of the tasks. It is probably best to use both methods: print statements to get an overall view of the execution and a debugger to observe the state at selected points.

Printing in Ada is done by using the services of the Text_IO package. The following three procedures should suffice:

Put(S) Prints the string S.

New_Line Sends the control sequence for a new line.

Put_Line(S) Like Put(S); New_Line.

Put(S) can be used several times to build up a line in pieces. Note that since the execution of tasks is interleaved, Put statements from several tasks may print on the same line. Put_Line will probably execute as an atomic operation.

To print numbers, an appropriate package must be created. This is done by compiling the following two-line program:

```
with Text_IO;
package Integer_Text_IO is new Integer_IO(Integer);
```

Then a context clause referencing Integer_Text_IO provides the procedures:

Put(N) Prints the integer N.

Put(N,W) Print the integer N in a field of width W.

Procedures from Text_IO and Integer_Text_IO may be combined in the same program as long as context clauses for both packages appear.

Experienced Ada programmers may prefer to use the **Image** function and string concatenation to prevent interleaving between two Put statements:

```
Put_Line("Ticket number = " & Integer'Image(Number(I));
```

The examples are written with infinite loops. Either replace them with terminating loops using `for`-clauses or make sure you know how to terminate a program that is looping (usually Control-C or Control-Break).

The examples were developed on the VAX Ada compiler from Digital Equipment Corporation. Implementation specific features of the VAX Ada compiler are:

- The package `Integer_Text_IO` is predefined and does not need to be compiled as stated above.

- Time-slicing is disabled unless explicitly enabled by a `pragma Time_Slice` clause.

- The standard suggests the use of a `pragma Shared` clause on global variables accessed by more than one task. Instead, VAX Ada supplies a `pragma Volatile` clause with slightly different semantics which should be used for these variables.

- In VAX Ada, both the time slice and the priority of a task can be changed during a debugging session.

The examples were also tested using the Alsys Ada compiler on a PC compatible computer. `pragma Shared` is supported by this implementation. To correctly execute the concurrent programming examples, the default parameters must be changed as follows:

```
default.bind(timer=>fast,slice=>10).
```

B.2   Common Memory

Figure B.1 shows a complete program for the first attempted solution to the mutual exclusion problem. It will only run on systems that implement time-slicing, otherwise the busy-wait loops will never terminate. The tasks are declared within a main procedure. The main procedure body is `null` since all the computation goes on in the dependent tasks. The main procedure will terminate when the dependent tasks terminate. Either add `for`-clauses to the loops in the task body or abort the program from the terminal.

This example will alternately print the message from each of the critical sections. If one of the idling sections is replaced by a very long computation, we can demonstrate how the other task is delayed in spite of lack of contention. The second attempt will deadlock after printing only one result. It will be difficult to demonstrate livelock and starvation since the time slice is long relative to the execution of the statements.

```
with Text_IO; use Text_IO;
procedure First is
   pragma Time_Slice(0.01);        -- VAX/Ada
   Turn: Integer := 1;
   pragma Volatile(Turn);          -- VAX/Ada

   task T1;
   task body T1 is
   begin
     loop
       Put_Line("Task 1 idling");
       loop exit when Turn = 1; end loop;
       Put_Line("Task 1 critical section");
       Turn := 2;
     end loop;
   end T1;

   task T2;
   task body T2 is
   begin
     loop
       Put_Line("Task 2 idling");
       loop exit when Turn = 2; end loop;
       Put_Line("Task 2 critical section");
       Turn := 1;
     end loop;
   end T2;
begin
   null;
end First;
```

Figure B.1 First attempt at mutual exclusion

B.3   Semaphores

Semaphores are implemented in a package which supplies both binary and general
semaphores (Figure B.2). The package must be mentioned in a context clause in
a program which uses it (Figure B.3). Since the semaphores are declared as task
types, data structures containing semaphores may be created.

The implementation of semaphores is standard (Figure B.4). For binary semaphores, successive **accept** statements are sufficient. We include them in a **select**
statement with a **terminate** alternative so that the user program can terminate.
Note that if Wait and Signal are not balanced, the task will not terminate. Since
entry queues are FIFO, this is an implementation of a blocked queue semaphore.

The general semaphore includes an initializing entry. A select statement accepts both Wait and Signal with a guard on the Wait to make sure that it does
not decrease the semaphore value below 0. Note that this is not a blocked queue
semaphore since there is no guarantee that the **select** will choose a Wait following
a Signal.

```
package Semaphore_Package is

  task type Binary_Semaphore is
    entry Wait;
    entry Signal;
  end Binary_Semaphore;

  task type Semaphore is
    entry Init(N: in Integer);
    entry Wait;
    entry Signal;
  end Semaphore;

end Semaphore_Package;
```

Figure B.2 Semaphore package specification

```
with Text_IO; use Text_IO;
with Semaphore_Package; use Semaphore_Package;
procedure Mutex is
  S: Binary_Semaphore;

  task T1;
  task body T1 is
  begin
    loop
      Put_Line("Task 1 is idling");
      S.Wait;
      Put_Line("Task 1 critical section");
      S.Signal;
    end loop;
  end T1;

  task T2;
  task body T2 is
  begin
    loop
      Put_Line("Task 2 is idling");
      S.Wait;
      Put_Line("Task 2 critical section");
      S.Signal;
    end loop;
  end T2;

begin
  null;
end Mutex;
```

Figure B.3 Mutual exclusion using semaphores

```
package body Semaphore_Package is

  task body Binary_Semaphore is
  begin
    loop
      select
        accept Wait;
        accept Signal;
      or
        terminate;
      end select;
    end loop;
  end Binary_Semaphore;

  task body Semaphore is
    Count: Integer;
  begin
    accept Init(N: Integer) do
      Count := N;
    end Init;
    loop
      select
        when Count > 0 =>
          accept Wait do
            Count := Count - 1;
          end Wait;
      or
        accept Signal do
          Count := Count + 1;
        end Signal;
      or
        terminate;
      end select;
    end loop;
  end Semaphore;

end Semaphore_Package;
```

Figure B.4 Implementation of semaphores

B.4 Monitors

Monitors are difficult to implement directly in Ada because there is no direct way of implementing condition variables by having a task leave a rendezvous, call another entry and then return to the original rendezvous. A close approximation is given in Figures B.5 and B.6. Figure B.5 supplies the tasking services to implement a monitor. Enter and Leave are essentially semaphores which control mutual exclusion to the monitor. Condition variables are implemented as task types providing the entries Signal and Wait. The function Non_Empty calls an additional entry in the condition task.

```
package Monitor_Package is
  task Monitor is
    entry Enter;
    entry Leave;
  end Monitor;

  task type Condition is
    entry Signal;
    entry Wait;
    entry Waiting(B: out Boolean);
  end Condition;

  function Non_Empty(C: Condition) return Boolean;
end Monitor_Package;
```

Figure B.5 Tasking services for a monitor

Using Monitor_Package one can write 'monitors' as packages. Figure B.6 shows the monitor for the producer–consumer which exports two procedures: Append and Take. Note that Enter and Leave have to be explicitly programmed – something that would normally be done implicitly by the monitor implementation. Signal is programmed to automatically release the monitor since it is restricted to be the last statement in a procedure. Now it is possible to write the program for the producer–consumer program using the monitor (Figure B.7). We have each task print the value of the elements produced and consumed so we can check that the program correctly preserves the order of the elements.

The implementation of mutual exclusion on a monitor is a simple binary semaphore (Figure B.8). The implementation of a condition variable is more difficult. If no processes are waiting, Signal simply releases mutual exclusion. If a process executes Wait, the condition task executes a nested accept Signal thereby blocking the waiting process until the condition is signaled. Since the signaling process holds mutual exclusion on the monitor, the awakened process automatically inherits the right to continue execution.

The code for the monitor package is complicated by the requirement that queries on Non_Empty always succeed. This is the reason for the loop within the accept Wait. If the queue status is queried, the select is re-issued. Only a rendezvous with Signal will exit the loop.

```
package Producer_Consumer_Monitor is
  procedure Append(V: in  Integer);
  procedure Take  (V: out Integer);
end Producer_Consumer_Monitor;

with Monitor_Package; use Monitor_Package;
package body Producer_Consumer_Monitor is
  Not_Empty, Not_Full: Condition;
  In_Ptr, Out_Ptr:      Integer := 0;
  Count:                Integer := 0;
  Buffer:               array(0..19) of Integer;

  procedure Append(V: in Integer) is
  begin
    Monitor.Enter;
    if Count = Buffer'Length then
        Monitor.Leave;
        Not_Full.Wait;
    end if;
    Buffer(In_Ptr) := V;
    In_Ptr := (In_Ptr + 1) mod Buffer'Length;
    Count := Count + 1;
    Not_Empty.Signal;
  end Append;

  procedure Take(V: out Integer) is
  begin
    Monitor.Enter;
    if Count = 0 then
      Monitor.Leave;
      Not_Empty.Wait;
    end if;
    V := Buffer(Out_Ptr);
    Out_Ptr := (Out_Ptr + 1) mod Buffer'Length;
    Count := Count - 1;
    Not_Full.Signal;
  end Take;
end Producer_Consumer_Monitor;
```

Figure B.6 Monitor for producer consumer

```
with Text_IO; use Text_IO;
with Integer_Text_IO;
with Producer_Consumer_Monitor; use Producer_Consumer_Monitor;
procedure Producer_Consumer is
  pragma Time_Slice(0.01);    -- VAX/Ada

  task Producer;
  task body Producer is
    N: Integer := 0;
  begin
    loop
      N := N + 1;
      Put("Produce  ");
      Integer_Text_IO.Put(N);
      New_Line;
      Append(N);
    end loop;
  end Producer;

  task Consumer;
  task body Consumer is
    N: Integer;
  begin
    loop
      Take(N);
      Put("Consume ");
      Integer_Text_IO.Put(N);
      New_Line;
    end loop;
  end Consumer;

begin
  null;
end Producer_Consumer;
```

Figure B.7 Producer consumer solution with monitors

```
package body Monitor_Package is

  function Non_empty(C: Condition) return Boolean is
    B: Boolean;
  begin
    C.Waiting(B);
    return B;
  end Non_empty;

  task body Monitor is
  begin
    loop
      accept Enter;
      accept Leave;
    end loop;
  end Monitor;

  task body Condition is
  begin
    loop
      select
        when Wait'Count = 0 =>
          accept Signal do Monitor.Leave; end Signal;
      or
        accept Wait do
          loop
            select
              accept Signal;
              exit;
            or
              accept Waiting(B: out Boolean) do
                B := True;
              end Waiting;
            end select;
          end loop;
        end Wait;
      or
        accept Waiting(B: out Boolean) do
          B := Wait'Count /= 0;
        end Waiting;
      end select;
    end loop;
  end Condition;

end Monitor_Package;
```

Figure B.8 Monitor package implementation

Appendix C

Implementation of the Ada Emulations

C.1 Introduction

This chapter presents the Ada emulations of occam and Linda. While the Linda emulation packages can be used with only the minimal knowledge of Ada required for this book, the occam emulation requires a sophisticated knowledge of the language.

C.2 occam

Aside from the prioritized alternate and repetitive alternate features, the concurrent programming primitives of occam are very similar to Ada and occam programs can be directly translated into Ada. However, to preserve the spirit of occam, an emulation should try to preserve the concept of 'channel' which is declared in a scope global to the communicating tasks rather than placing the declaration of the entries in the accepting task. In the case of the matrix multiplication example, the tasks around the boundary of the matrix (8 out of 9 in the example) would require special programming.

We have developed a way to emulate occam channels as Ada tasks so that the computational tasks can all be of the same type. Unfortunately, this requires a non-trivial data structure and initialization scheme which must be created separately for each new problem. The matrix multiplication example is given in full detail and can be used as a model for solving other problems.

Each channel is declared as an additional task with an entry named Output. The process executing an occam Output statement can simply call this entry in the channel task. The problem is with processes executing occam Input statements. We want to allow them to execute select statements. Thus the channel tasks must *call* entries in the accepting tasks. In Ada, this requires that the channel task know the name of the accepting task and the entry name. This is accomplished during initialization of the channel task. The problem is that it is impossible to pass a 'task' as a parameter. We can only pass a pointer to a specific task type.

Rather than have different code for each channel,[1] we use variant records to pass a pointer to a general task type. The variant record and the channel code will need modification for each problem, but this is not difficult to do.

We give the complete listing of the matrix multiplication program which can be used as a guide to writing other emulations. The main program (Figure C.1) declares all the tasks and channels. `Task_Types` has a value for each type of task in the program and is used as the discriminant in the variant record `Tasks`. This variant record assumes a transputer-like solution where every process uses at most four channels which are initialized with channel indices. The varying part contains a field for the task.

The channels are numbered sequentially and the `Configure` procedure assigns channel indices to each of the tasks. The computations are detailed but not difficult if following on a diagram (Figure C.2). Initialization is done by calling the `Init` entry of each task with a pointer to the data structure of type `Tasks`. The task stores its channel indices and calls the `Destination` entry of each outgoing channel to configure the channel.

The channel task body (Figure C.3) stores the task pointer and the channel index. It then suspends on a **select** statement waiting for some process to execute an output statement. The **select** has a **terminate** alternative so that the channels can terminate once the processes themselves have done so. Once a value has been received, the channel stores it and then calls the destination process. A **case** statement on the discriminant of task record is used to call the correct task and the channel index is used as an index in an entry family. Calls to tasks which are not destinations of any channel cause an exception to be raised.

While the configuration of the system is extremely difficult, the programming of the processes themselves is straightforward (Figure C.4).

---

[1] More precisely, for each channel calling a different destination task type.

```
procedure Matrix is

  type Task_Types is (Multiplier, Source, Sink, Zero, Result);

  Size: constant Integer := 3;
  type Vector is array(1..Size) of Integer;
  Matrix1: array(1..Size) of Vector :=
    ((1,2,3),(4,5,6),(7,8,9));
  Matrix2: array(1..Size) of Vector :=
    ((1,0,2),(0,1,2),(1,0,0));

  type Channels is range 1..2*Size*(Size+1)+1;

  type Tasks(Task_Type: Task_Types);
  type Task_Ptr is access Tasks;

  task type Multiplier_Task is
    entry Init(Coeff: Integer; T: Task_Ptr);
    entry Input (Channels)(I: in  Integer);
  end Multiplier_Task;

  task type Source_Task is
    entry Init(V: Vector; T: Task_Ptr);
  end Source_Task;

  task type Sink_Task is
    entry Init(T: Task_Ptr);
    entry Input (Channels)(I: in  Integer);
  end Sink_Task;

  task type Zero_Task is
    entry Init(T: Task_Ptr);
  end Zero_Task;

  task type Result_Task is
    entry Init(ID: Integer; T: Task_Ptr);
    entry Input (Channels)(I: in  Integer);
  end Result_Task;

  type Tasks(Task_Type: Task_Types) is
    record
      North, East, South, West: Channels;
      case Task_Type is
        when Multiplier => M: Multiplier_Task;
        when Source     => S: Source_Task;
        when Sink       => T: Sink_Task;
        when Zero       => Z: Zero_Task;
        when Result     => R: Result_Task;
      end case;
    end record;
```

Figure C.1 Main program for matrix multiplication

```
task type Channel_Task is
  entry Destination(T_Ptr: Task_Ptr; Chan: Channels);
  entry Output(I: in Integer);
end Channel_Task;

M: array(1..Size, 1..Size) of Task_Ptr;
S: array(1..Size) of Task_Ptr;
T: array(1..Size) of Task_Ptr;
Z: array(1..Size) of Task_Ptr;
R: array(1..Size) of Task_Ptr;

Channel: array(Channels range 1..Channels'Last-1) of Channel_Task;

task body Multiplier_Task is separate;
task body Source_Task    is separate;
task body Sink_Task      is separate;
task body Zero_Task      is separate;
task body Result_Task    is separate;
task body Channel_Task   is separate;

procedure Activate is
begin
  M := (others => (others => new Tasks(Multiplier)));
  S := (others => new Tasks(Source));
  T := (others => new Tasks(Sink));
  Z := (others => new Tasks(Zero));
  R := (others => new Tasks(Result));
end Activate;

procedure Configure is
  N: Channels;
begin
  N := 1;
  for I in 1..Size loop
    S(I).South := N;  M(1,I).North    := N;
    N := N + 1;
    Z(I).West  := N;  M(I,Size).East  := N;
    N := N + 1; ·
    T(I).North := N;  M(Size,I).South := N;
    N := N + 1;
    R(I).East  := N;  M(I,1).West     := N;
    N := N + 1;
    for J in 2..Size loop
      M(I,J).West := N;  M(I,J-1).East := N;
      N := N + 1;
    end loop;
    if I /= Size then
      for J in 1..Size loop
        M(I,J).South := N;  M(I+1,J).North := N;
        N := N + 1;
      end loop;
    end if;
  end loop;
end Configure;
```

Figure C.1 Main program for matrix multiplication (*continued*)

```
procedure Init is
begin
  for I in 1..Size loop
    R(I).R.Init(I, R(I));
    S(I).S.Init(Matrix2(I), S(I));
    T(I).T.Init(T(I));
    Z(I).Z.Init(Z(I));
    for J in 1..Size loop
      M(I,J).M.Init(Matrix1(I)(J), M(I,J));
    end loop;
  end loop;
end Init;

begin
  Activate;
  Configure;
  Init;
end Matrix;
```

Figure C.1 Main program for matrix multiplication (*continued*)

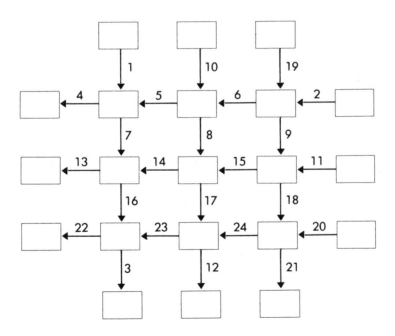

Figure C.2 Assignment of channels to processes

```
separate(Matrix)
task body Channel_Task is
  T:  Task_Ptr;
  Ch: Channels;
  Save: Integer;
  Invalid_Channel: exception;
begin
  accept Destination(T_Ptr: Task_Ptr; Chan: Channels) do
    T  := T_Ptr;
    Ch := Chan;
  end Destination;
  loop
    select
      accept Output(I: in Integer) do
        Save := I;
      end Output;
    or
      terminate;
    end select;
    case T.Task_Type is
      when Multiplier => T.M.Input(Ch)(Save);
      when Source     => raise Invalid_Channel;
      when Sink       => T.T.Input(Ch)(Save);
      when Zero       => raise Invalid_Channel;
      when Result     => T.R.Input(Ch)(Save);
    end case;
  end loop;
end Channel_Task;
```

Figure C.3 Channel task

```
separate(Matrix)
task body Multiplier_Task is
  North, East, South, West: Channels;
  X, Sum, A: Integer;
begin
  accept Init(Coeff: Integer; T: Task_Ptr) do
    A := Coeff;
    North := T.North; East := T.East;
    South := T.South; West := T.West;
    Channel(North).Destination(T, T.North);
    Channel(East) .Destination(T, T.East);
  end Init;
  for N in 1..Size loop
      accept Input(North)(I: in Integer) do
        X := I;
      end Input;
      Channel(South).Output(X);
      accept Input(East) (I: in Integer) do
        Sum := I;
      end Input;
      Sum := Sum + A*X;
      Channel(West).Output(Sum);
  end loop;
end Multiplier_Task;

separate(Matrix)
task body Source_Task is
  South: Channels;
  Vec: Vector;
begin
  accept Init(V: Vector; T: Task_Ptr) do
    Vec := V;    South := T.South;
  end Init;
  for N in 1..Size loop
    Channel(South).Output(Vec(N));
  end loop;
end Source_Task;

separate(Matrix)
task body Sink_Task is
  North: Channels;
begin
  accept Init(T: Task_Ptr) do
    North := T.North;
    Channel(North).Destination(T, T.North);
  end Init;
  for N in 1..Size loop
    accept Input(North)(I: in Integer);
  end loop;
end Sink_Task;
```

Figure C.4 Tasks for occam matrix multiplication

```
separate(Matrix)
task body Zero_Task is
  West: Channels;
begin
  accept Init(T: Task_Ptr) do
    West := T.West;
  end Init;
  for N in 1..Size loop
    Channel(West).Output(0);
  end loop;
end Zero_Task;

with Text_IO; use Text_IO;
with Integer_Text_IO; use Integer_Text_IO;
separate(Matrix)
task body Result_Task is
  East: Channels;
  Ident: Integer;
begin
  accept Init(ID: Integer; T: Task_Ptr) do
    Ident := ID;  East := T.East;
    Channel(East).Destination(T, T.East);
  end Init;
  for N in 1..Size loop
    accept Input(East)(I: in Integer) do
      Put(Ident); Put(N); Put(I); New_Line;
    end Input;
  end loop;
end Result_Task;
```

Figure C.4 Tasks for occam matrix multiplication (*continued*)

C.3   Linda

Two packages have been written to embed Linda primitives in Ada. Tuple_Defs creates and accesses tuples and Tuple_Package manages the tuple space. Figure C.5 contains the specification of package Tuple_Defs. A user of the package need only know that there exist types Tuple_Element and Tuple and functions that convert from these types to ordinary data types.

Vector is an unconstrained array of integers used in the matrix multiplication example. Tuples can consist of a sequence of one to four values of type Tuple_Element. Each of these can be of types: Integer, Character, Boolean, String, Vector. Formal values are defined which can be used in the creation of tuples. Finally, conversion routines convert ordinary values to tuple elements and conversely, extract values from tuples. The extraction functions take a index denoting the element to be extracted.

```
package Tuple_Defs is

  type Vector   is array(Positive range <>) of Integer;

  type Int_Ptr  is access Integer;
  type Char_Ptr is access Character;
  type Bool_Ptr is access Boolean;
  type Str_Ptr  is access String;
  type Vec_Ptr  is access Vector;

  type Tuple_Types is (None, Ints, Chars, Bools, Strs, Vecs);

  type Tuple_Element(Tuple_Type: Tuple_Types := None) is
    record
      case Tuple_Type is
        when None => null;
        when Ints  => I: Int_Ptr;
        when Chars => C: Char_Ptr;
        when Bools => B: Bool_Ptr;
        when Strs  => S: Str_Ptr;
        when Vecs  => V: Vec_Ptr;
      end case;
    end record;

  Null_Element: constant Tuple_Element:=(Tuple_Type=>None);

  Formal_Int:   constant Tuple_Element := (Ints,  null);
  Formal_Char:  constant Tuple_Element := (Chars, null);
  Formal_Bool:  constant Tuple_Element := (Bools, null);
  Formal_Str:   constant Tuple_Element := (Strs,  null);
  Formal_Vec:   constant Tuple_Element := (Vecs,  null);

  type Tuples is array(1..4) of Tuple_Element;

  Null_Tuple: constant Tuples:=(others=>(Tuple_Type=>None));

  function Int(I:  Integer)   return Tuple_Element;
  function Char(C: Character) return Tuple_Element;
  function Bool(B: Boolean)   return Tuple_Element;
  function Str(S:  String)    return Tuple_Element;
  function Vec(V:  Vector)    return Tuple_Element;

  function Int(T:  Tuples; Index: Integer) return Integer;
  function Char(T: Tuples; Index: Integer) return Character;
  function Bool(T: Tuples; Index: Integer) return Boolean;
  function Str(T:  Tuples; Index: Integer) return String;
  function Vec(T:  Tuples; Index: Integer) return Vector;

  function Create_Tuple(T1, T2, T3, T4: Tuple_Element :=
        (Null_Element)) return Tuples;
  function Match(T1, T2: Tuples) return Boolean;

end Tuple_Defs;
```

Figure C.5 Tuple definitions

```
package Tuple_Package is

   function  Input (T: Tuples) return Tuples;
   function  Read  (T: Tuples) return Tuples;
   procedure Output(T: Tuples);

   function  Input (T1, T2, T3, T4: Tuple_Element :=
         Null_Element) return Tuples;
   function  Read  (T1, T2, T3, T4: Tuple_Element :=
         Null_Element) return Tuples;
   procedure Output(T1, T2, T3, T4: Tuple_Element :=
         Null_Element);

end Tuple_Package;
```

Figure C.6 Tuple Space package

The package Tuple_Package defines the Linda primitives (Figure C.6). Each primitive can take one to four elements as parameters or an entire tuple. Input and Read are functions which return a matching tuple.

```
with Text_IO; use Text_IO;
with Integer_Text_IO; use Integer_Text_IO;
with Tuple_Defs; use Tuple_Defs;
with Tuple_Package; use Tuple_Package;
procedure Matrix is
  Result: Tuples;
  task type Workers;
  Worker: array(1..2) of Workers;
  task body Workers is separate;

begin
  Output(Char('A'), Int(1), Vec((1,2,3)));
  Output(Char('A'), Int(2), Vec((4,5,6)));
  Output(Char('A'), Int(3), Vec((7,8,9)));
  Output(Char('B'), Int(1), Vec((1,0,1)));
  Output(Char('B'), Int(2), Vec((0,1,0)));
  Output(Char('B'), Int(3), Vec((2,2,0)));
  Output(Char('N'), Int(1));

  Put_Line(" Row    Col    Result");
  for I in 1..3 loop
    for J in 1..3 loop
      Result := Input(Char('C'), Int(I), Int(J), Formal_Int);
      Put(I,4); Put(J,6); Put(Int(Result,4),8); New_Line;
    end loop;
  end loop;
end Matrix;
```

Figure C.7 Matrix multiplication main program

The main program for matrix multiplication is very simple (Figure C.7). It creates the matrix row and column tuples, initializes the task counter and then reaps the result tuples. Note the use of the conversion functions to create tuple elements from ordinary values and the use of the formal integer tuple element when reading the result. The example shows two worker tasks, but this is trivial to modify by changing the array declaration. The worker tasks are shown in Figure C.8. The extraction functions are used in the computation of the inner product to extract values from the tuple.

```
separate(Matrix)
task body Workers is
  Next, Row_Tuple, Col_Tuple: Tuples;
  Element, I, J, Sum: Integer;
begin
  loop
    Next := Input(Char('N'), Formal_Int);
    Element := Int(Next, 2);
    Output(Char('N'), Int(Element+1));
    exit when Element > 3 * 3;
    I := (Element - 1)  / 3 + 1;
    J := (Element - 1) mod 3 + 1;
    Row_Tuple := Read(Char('A'), Int(I), Formal_Vec);
    Col_Tuple := Read(Char('B'), Int(J), Formal_Vec);

    Sum := 0;
    for N in 1..3 loop
      Sum := Sum + Vec(Row_Tuple,3)(N) * Vec(Col_Tuple,3)(N);
    end loop;

    Output(Char('C'), Int(I), Int(J), Int(Sum));
  end loop;
end Workers;
```

Figure C.8 Worker tasks for matrix multiplication

As shown above, a familiarity with essential points of the package specifications suffices to write programs that emulate Linda. The rest of the section contains information on the implementation of the emulation.

Tuple elements are implemented by variant records each of which contains a pointer to the element value (Figure C.5). A null pointer denotes a formal tuple element. A tuple is a fixed length array of tuple elements where unused elements are filled with the null element. Note that Create_Tuple is not used in the matrix multiplication example since the Linda primitives have been defined to take sequences of tuples and call Create_Tuple themselves (Figure C.6). Function Match is used internally by the tuple space manager. The body of Tuple_Defs is straightforward (Figure C.9). The only non-trivial part is matching tuple elements which must be done on a case by case basis for each type.

```
package body Tuple_Defs is

   function Int(I: Integer) return Tuple_Element is
   begin
     return (Ints, new Integer'(I));
   end Int;

   function Char(C: Character) return Tuple_Element is
   begin
     return (Chars, new Character'(C));
   end Char;

   function Bool(B: Boolean) return Tuple_Element is
   begin
     return (Bools, new Boolean'(B));
   end Bool;

   function Str(S: String) return Tuple_Element is
   begin
     return (Strs, new String'(S));
   end Str;

   function Vec(V: Vector) return Tuple_Element is
   begin
     return (Vecs, new Vector'(V));
   end Vec;

   function Int(T: Tuples; Index: Integer) return Integer is
   begin
     return T(Index).I.all;
   end Int;

   function Char(T: Tuples; Index: Integer) return Character is
   begin
     return T(Index).C.all;
   end Char;

   function Bool(T: Tuples; Index: Integer) return Boolean is
   begin
     return T(Index).B.all;
   end Bool;

   function Str(T: Tuples; Index: Integer) return String is
   begin
     return T(Index).S.all;
   end Str;

   function Vec(T: Tuples; Index: Integer) return Vector is
   begin
     return T(Index).V.all;
   end Vec;
```

Figure C.9 Tuple definitions package body

```
    function Create_Tuple(T1, T2, T3, T4: Tuple_Element :=
        (Null_Element)) return Tuples is
    begin
      return (T1, T2, T3, T4);
    end Create_Tuple;

    function Element_Match(E1, E2: Tuple_Element)
        return Boolean is
    begin
      case E1.Tuple_Type is
        when None => return True;
        when Ints =>
          return E1=Formal_Int  or else E2=Formal_Int  or else
              E1.I.all = E2.I.all;
        when Chars =>
          return E1=Formal_Char or else E2=Formal_Char or else
              E1.C.all = E2.C.all;
        when Bools =>
          return E1=Formal_Bool or else E2=Formal_Bool or else
              E1.B.all = E2.B.all;
        when Strs =>
          return E1=Formal_Str  or else E2=Formal_Str  or else
              E1.S.all = E2.S.all;
        when Vecs =>
          return E1=Formal_Vec  or else E2=Formal_Vec  or else
              E1.V.all = E2.V.all;
      end case;
    end Element_Match;

    function Match(T1, T2: Tuples) return Boolean is
    begin
      for J in Tuples'Range loop
        if T1(J).Tuple_Type /= T2(J).Tuple_Type
                or else
            not Element_Match(T1(J), T2(J)) then
              return False;
        end if;
      end loop;
      return True;
    end Match;
  end Tuple_Defs;
```

Figure C.9 Tuple definitions package body (*continued*)

Package Tuple_Package (Figures C.6 and C.10) contains the TS which is a fixed array of tuples. An exception is defined if TS is full. Tasks are declared which are responsible for mutual exclusion to the TS and for blocking Input and Read requests if the tuple is not available. There are two versions of each primitive: one which takes a tuple parameter and the other which takes a sequence of tuple values. Non-blocking primitives are not implemented.

```
with Tuple_Defs; use Tuple_Defs;
package body Tuple_Package is

  Tuple_Space: array(0..50) of Tuples :=
      (others => Null_Tuple);
  Out_of_Tuple_Space: exception;

  task Space_Lock is
    entry Lock;
    entry Unlock;
  end Space_Lock;

  task Suspend is
    entry Release;
    entry Notify;
    entry Request;
  end Suspend;

  task body Space_Lock is separate;
  task body Suspend    is separate;

  function Find_Tuple(T: in Tuples) return Integer is
  begin
    Tuple_Space(0) := T;
    for I in reverse Tuple_Space'Range loop
      if Match(T, Tuple_Space(I)) then return I; end if;
    end loop;
  end Find_Tuple;

function Find_Tuple_or_Suspend(T: Tuples; Remove: Boolean)
    return Tuples is
  T1: Tuples;
  I: Integer;
begin
  loop
    Space_Lock.Lock;
    I := Find_Tuple(T);
    if I /= 0 then
      T1 := Tuple_Space(I);
      if Remove then Tuple_Space(I):=Null_Tuple; end if;
      Space_Lock.Unlock;
      return T1;
    else
      Suspend.Notify;
      Suspend.Request;
    end if;
  end loop;
end Find_Tuple_or_Suspend;
```

Figure C.10 Body of Tuple Space package

```ada
          procedure Output(T: Tuples) is
            I: Integer;
          begin
            Space_Lock.Lock;
            I := Find_Tuple(Null_Tuple);
            if I = 0 then raise Out_of_Tuple_Space; end if;
            Tuple_Space(I) := T;
            Suspend.Release;
          end Output;

          procedure Output (T1, T2, T3, T4: Tuple_Element :=
             Null_Element) is
          begin
            Output(Create_Tuple(T1, T2, T3, T4));
          end Output;

          function Input(T: Tuples) return Tuples is
          begin
            return Find_Tuple_or_Suspend(T, Remove => True);
          end Input;

          function  Input  (T1, T2, T3, T4: Tuple_Element :=
             Null_Element) return Tuples is
          begin
             return Input(Create_Tuple(T1, T2, T3, T4));
           end Input;

          function Read(T: Tuples) return Tuples is
          begin
            return Find_Tuple_or_Suspend(T, Remove => False);
          end Read;

          function  Read(T1, T2, T3, T4: Tuple_Element :=
             Null_Element) return Tuples is
          begin
             return Read(Create_Tuple(T1, T2, T3, T4));
          end Read;

      end Tuple_Package;
```

Figure C.10 Body of Tuple Space package (*continued*)

Output searches for a null tuple in TS and replaces it with the parameter. Input and Read search for a matching tuple. If found, it can be returned (and deleted for Input). If not, the process suspends. The reason for the two-instruction suspend will be described when the task body for Suspend is shown.

The tuple space uses two tasks (Figure C.11). Task Space_Lock implements a semaphore to ensure that only one task accesses TS at any time.

Suspension on non-existing tuples is difficult. We decide that every Output instruction will awaken all suspended processes which then proceed to try to

```
separate(Tuple_Package)
task body Space_Lock is
begin
  loop
    select
      accept Lock;
      accept Unlock;
    or
      terminate;
    end select;
  end loop;
end Space_Lock;

separate(Tuple_Package)
task body Suspend is
  Suspended: Integer := 0;
begin
  loop
    select
      accept Release;
      for I in 1..Suspended loop
        accept Request;
      end loop;
      Suspended := 0;
    or
      accept Notify;
      Suspended := Suspended + 1;
    or
      terminate;
    end select;
    Space_Lock.Unlock;
  end loop;
end Suspend;
```

Figure C.11 Tuple Space tasks

match the new tuple, suspending themselves again if necessary. The problem is how do we know how many processes must be awakened? The obvious way to do this is to have Output call an entry, here named Release, which will then loop accepting all of the Request'Count processes which are suspended. It is clear that a suspended process must have unlocked TS before calling the Request entry, otherwise no other process could ever execute Output. We have to watch out for the following scenario:

1. Initially no processes suspended and empty TS.
2. P1 executes Input and locks TS.
3. P1 does not find the required tuple.
4. P1 unlocks TS.
5. P2 executes Output with matching tuple and locks TS.
6. P2 notes that no processes are suspended.

7. P2 unlocks TS.
8. P1 suspends waiting for a tuple that is actually there.

The solution is to have suspended processes make an initial call to the Suspend task to Notify that it will suspend. Since this is executed while holding the lock, the count of suspended processes will always be correct. There is no problem holding the lock, because the accept body is empty and will never block the calling task. Notify will release the lock on the TS which will allow processes to execute Output and find out exactly how many processes are suspended. Note that the solution works because Input and Read use simple entry calls without timeouts.

Termination of tasks in a library package such as Tuple_Package is not defined in the standard though the VAX Ada implementation will terminate these two tasks. If problems occur on other compilers, Tuple_Package can be declared as a local package within the main program.

Appendix D

Distributed Algorithms in Ada

D.1 Introduction

In this appendix we present the details of an Ada implementation of distributed algorithms that is suitable for laboratory experimentation. It has been used to implement the Ricart–Agrawala algorithm for distributed mutual exclusion, the DS and TM algorithms for distributed termination and the snapshot algorithm. The complete code of the TM algorithm will be given followed by discussion of the other algorithms. Not included will be the Put_Line statements scattered throughout the code to instrument the program.

D.2 The TM Algorithm

The nodes of the distributed system are declared as an array of tasks, one task per node. Communications among the nodes can be done simply by indexing the node ID and calling the Message or Signal entry. The main process is declared as a subtask within the node task. The permits concurrency between the main process and the communications process yet allows them to access the same global variables declared in the node task. They cannot both be tasks in a package because it is not possible to create a data structure of packages to index the nodes. The main process must be a subtask of the communications task and not conversely because accept statements must appear in the outermost level of a task.

Figure D.1 shows the outer framework of the program. Each node has two entries for initialization purposes. The first is used to give a node its ID and the number of incoming and outgoing edges. Then the node executes an accept Configure statement for each edge. It is passed the ID of the task at the other end of the edge. Entry calls in the main program (Figure D.2) construct the node topology. Once configuration is complete, Main_Process can be initiated and the main loop entered.

```
with Semaphore_Package; use Semaphore_Package;
procedure TM is
  type Node_Count is range 0..4;
  subtype Node_ID is Node_Count range 1..Node_Count'Last;

  task type Nodes is
    entry Init(ID: Node_ID; N_I, N_O: Node_Count);
    entry Configure(C: Node_ID);
    entry Message(M: Integer; ID: Node_ID);
    entry Signal(ID: Node_ID);
  end Nodes;
  Node: array(Node_ID) of Nodes;

  task body Nodes is
    -- Global variables
    -- Main Process task
  begin
    accept Init(ID: Node_ID; N_I, N_O: Node_Count) do
      I := ID;
      N_In  := N_I;
      N_Out := N_O;
    end Init;
    for J in 1..N_In loop
      accept Configure(C: Node_ID) do
        Incoming(C).Exists := True;
      end Configure;
    end loop;
    for J in 1..N_Out loop
      accept Configure(C: Node_ID) do
        Outgoing(C).Exists := True;
      end Configure;
    end loop;
    Main_Process.Init;

    -- Main loop
  end Nodes;
begin
  -- Configure node topology
end TM;
```

Figure D.1 Framework of TM algorithm

The global variables are shown in Figure D.3.[1] The only additions to the declarations shown in the description of the algorithm are the variables N_In and N_Out which are used during configuration only. The main loop of the node process is straightforward (Figure D.4). A **terminate** alternative has been added to the **select** statement. When Main_Process terminates, the node task will

---

[1] In VAX Ada global variables used by several processes should be declared with **pragma Volatile**.

```
Node(1).Init(1,0,2);
Node(1).Configure(2); Node(1).Configure(3);

Node(2).Init(2,2,2);
Node(2).Configure(1); Node(2).Configure(3);
Node(2).Configure(3); Node(2).Configure(4);

Node(3).Init(3,3,1);
Node(3).Configure(1); Node(3).Configure(2);
Node(3).Configure(4); Node(3).Configure(2);

Node(4).Init(4,1,1);
Node(4).Configure(2); Node(4).Configure(3);
```

Figure D.2 Configure node topology

```
type Edge is
  record
    Exists:  Boolean := False;
    Active:  Boolean := False;
    Marker_Received: Boolean := False;
  end record;

Incoming: array(Node_ID) of Edge;
Outgoing: array(Node_ID) of Edge;
N_In, N_Out: Node_Count := 0;

First_Edge:  Node_Count := 0;
N_Signals:   Natural := 0;

I: Node_ID;
S: Binary_Semaphore := Init(1);
Received_ID: Node_ID;
Received_Data: Integer;
```

Figure D.3 Global variables

also be able to terminate since all its sibling node tasks will eventually be waiting on the **terminate** alternative. **Main_Process** (Figure D.5) has an initiate entry to prevent it from commencing execution until the node process completes the configuration of the global variables.

There is a difference between the the processing done in the source node and the processing done in other nodes. The source node sends two messages followed by a marker on each outgoing channel. Then it simply waits for termination. Internal nodes go through the following stages:

1. Wait to be engaged (a message has been received on **First_Edge**).

2. Send five messages on each outgoing channel.

3. Wait for a marker on **First_Edge**.

```
loop
  select
    accept Message(M: Integer; ID: Node_ID) do
      Received_ID := ID;
      Received_Data := M;
    end Message;
    if Received_Data < 0 then
      Incoming(Received_ID).Marker_Received := True;
    else
      if First_Edge = 0 then
        First_Edge := Received_ID;
      end if;
    end if;
    if not Incoming(Received_ID).Active then
      Incoming(Received_ID).Active := True;
    end if;
  or
    accept Signal(ID: Node_ID) do
      Received_ID := ID;
    end Signal;
    Outgoing(Received_ID).Active := False;
    Wait(S);
    N_Signals := N_Signals - 1;
    Signal(S);
  or
    terminate;
  end select;
end loop;
```

Figure D.4 Main loop of communications task

4. Send markers on each outgoing channel.

5. Wait for marker on each incoming channel.

6. Execute the `Decide_to_Terminate` function until successful and then terminate.

To demonstrate the algorithms, it was assumed that each node sends each message on all outgoing channels, so a loop over all existing outgoing channels is programmed in `Send_Message` (Figure D.6).

`Received_Markers` (Figure D.7) is straightforward – checking if markers have been received from each incoming channel. `Decide_to_Terminate` (Figure D.8) has been discussed in Chapter 12.

```
task Main_Process is
  entry Init;
end Main_Process;

task body Main_Process is
  Count: Integer := 0;
  Markers_Sent: Boolean := False;
begin
  accept Init;
  if I = 1 then
    Send_Messages(Count);
    Send_Messages(Count);
    Send_Messages(-1);
    loop
      exit when Decide_to_Terminate;
    end loop;
  else
    loop
      if Count < 5 then
        if First_Edge /= 0 then
          Count := Count + 1;
          Send_Messages(Count);
        end if;
      elsif not Markers_Sent then
        if Incoming(First_Edge).Marker_Received then
          Send_Messages(-1);
          Markers_Sent := True;
        end if;
      elsif Received_Markers then
          loop
            exit when Decide_to_Terminate;
          end loop;
          exit;
      end if;
    end loop;
  end if;
end Main_Process;
```

Figure D.5 Main process task

```
procedure Send_Messages(Data: Integer) is
begin
  for J in Node_ID loop
    if Outgoing(J).Exists then
      if not Outgoing(J).Active then
        Outgoing(J).Active := True;
        Wait(S);
        N_Signals := N_Signals + 1;
        Signal(S);
      end if;
      Node(J).Message(Data, I);
    end if;
  end loop;
end Send_Messages;
```

Figure D.6 Sending messages

```
function Received_Markers return Boolean is
begin
  for J in Node_ID loop
    if Incoming(J).Exists and then
      not Incoming(J).Marker_Received then
        return False;
    end if;
  end loop;
  return True;
end Received_Markers;
```

Figure D.7 Receiving markers

```
function Decide_to_Terminate return Boolean is
  procedure Send_Signals(ID: Node_ID) is
  begin
    Node(ID).Signal(I);
    Incoming(ID).Active := False;
  end Send_Signals;

begin
  for J in Node_ID loop
    if   J /= First_Edge and then
         Incoming(J).Active then
           Send_Signals(J);
    end if;
  end loop;

  if N_Signals = 0 then
    if I = 1 then
      null;
    elsif First_Edge /= 0 then
      Send_Signals(First_Edge);
      First_Edge := 0;
    end if;
    return True;
  else
    return False;
  end if;
end Decide_to_Terminate;
```

Figure D.8 Checking for termination

D.3   The Ricart–Agrawala Algorithm

This algorithm for distributed mutual exclusion can be implemented exactly as
described in Chapter 11 or it can fit into the paradigm described here. Instead of
three tasks, the request and reply tasks are converted into a node communications
task which contains the main process as a subtask (Figure D.9). When compared
with the distributed termination algorithms, the mutual exclusion algorithm is
simpler because the process graph must be complete, each process connected
to each other. Thus we can dispense with the Incoming and Outgoing data
structures. Finally, each main process makes a constant number of entries to the
critical section and then terminates. The terminate alternative allows the node
processes to terminate.

```
procedure RA is
  task type Nodes is
    entry Init(ID: Node_ID);
    entry Request_Message(Num: Integer; ID: Node_ID);
    entry Reply_Message;
  end Nodes;
  Node: array(Node_ID) of Nodes;

  task body Nodes is
    -- Global variables
    -- Main process
  begin
    accept Init(ID: Node_ID) do
      I := ID;
      Main_Process.Init;
    end Init;
    loop
      select
        accept Request_Message(Num: Integer; ID: Node_ID) do
          Received_Number := Num;
          Received_ID     := ID;
        end Request_Message;
        Received_Request;
      or
        accept Reply_Message;
        Received_Reply;
      or
        terminate;
      end select;
    end loop;
  end Nodes;
begin
  for J in 1..N loop
    Node(J).Init(J);
  end loop;
end RA;
```

Figure D.9 Distributed mutual exclusion

D.4   The Dijkstra–Scholten Algorithm

The main process of the DS algorithm implementation is shown in Figure D.10. The source process sends two messages on all outgoing nodes while the internal processes send up to five messages. The source process will terminate upon receiving a final signal. However, the internal processes may be repeatedly disengaged and re-engaged as new messages come in. This is modeled by having the process execute Decide_to_Terminate after sending each message and then checking if First_Edge still indicates that the process is engaged. Thus internal nodes will not terminate and the execution of the program must be manually interrupted.

```
task body Main_Process is
  Count: Integer := 0;
begin
  accept Init;
  if I = 1 then
    Send_Messages;
    Send_Messages;
    loop
      exit when Decide_to_Terminate;
    end loop;
  else
    loop
      loop
        exit when First_Edge /= 0;
      end loop;
      if Count < 5 then
        Count := Count + 1;
        Send_Messages;
      end if;
      loop
        exit when not Decide_to_Terminate or First_Edge /= 0;
      end loop;
    end loop;
  end if;
end Main_Process;
```

Figure D.10 Main process of DS algorithm

D.5   Snapshots

The implementation of the snapshot algorithm is straightforward except for printing the answers. The main process (Figure D.11) sends messages and occasionally initiates spontaneous recording of the state. When all messages have been sent, the main process waits in a loop until State_Recorded is true and markers have been received on all incoming channels. Then it prints the recorded state. As a final detail, an additional semaphore Print (which is global to all nodes) is used so that the lines of printing from the nodes do not interleave.

```
task body Main_Process is
  function Write_State return Boolean is
  begin
    if not State_Recorded then return False; end if;
    for J in Node_ID loop
      if Incoming(J).Exists and not Incoming(J).Marker_Passed then
        return False;
      end if; ,
    end loop;
    Wait(Print);
    -- Print state of this node
    Signal(Print);
    return True;
  end Write_State;

begin
  accept Init;
  for J in 1..9 loop
    Send_Messages(J);
    case I is
      when 2 | 3 => null;
      when 1 => if J = 6 then Record_State; end if;
      when 4 => if J = 3 then Record_State; end if;
    end case;
  end loop;
  loop exit when Write_State; end loop;
end Main_Process;
```

Figure D.11 Main process of snapshot algorithm

Bibliography

[ACG86]   S. Ahuja, N. Carriero, and D. Gelernter. Linda and friends. *IEEE Computer*, 19(8): 26–34, 1986.

[Bar89]   J.G.P. Barnes. *Programming in Ada*. Addison-Wesley, Reading, MA, 1989.

[Ben84]   M. Ben-Ari. Algorithms for on-the-fly garbage collection. *ACM Trans. Program. Lang. and Syst.*, 6(3): 333–44, 1984.

[BEW88]   D. Bustard, J. Elder, and J. Welsh. *Concurrent Programming Structures*. Prentice Hall International, Hemel Hempstead, 1988.

[BH77]   P. Brinch Hansen. *The Architecture of Concurrent Programs*. Prentice Hall, Englewood Cliffs, NJ, 1977.

[Boo83]   G. Booch. *Software Engineering with Ada*. Benjamin/Cummings, Menlo Park, CA, 1983.

[BR85]   T.P. Baker and G.A. Riccardi. Ada tasking: From semantics to efficient implementation. *IEEE Software*, 2(2): 34–46, 1985.

[Bur85]   A. Burns. *Concurrent Programming in Ada*. Cambridge University Press, Cambridge, 1985.

[CDJ84]   F.B. Chambers, D.A. Duce, and G.P. Jones (eds). *Distributed Computing*. Academic Press, London, 1984.

[CG89]   N. Carriero and D. Gelernter. How to write parallel programs: a guide to the perplexed. *ACM Computing Surveys* (forthcoming).

[CL85]   K.M. Chandy and L. Lamport. Distributed snapshots: determining global states of distributed systems. *ACM Trans. Computer Syst.*, 3(1): 63–75, 1985.

[CM84]   K.M. Chandy and J. Misra. The drinking philosophers problem. *ACM Trans. Program. Lang. and Syst.*, 6(4): 632–46, 1984.

[CM88]   K.M. Chandy and J. Misra. *Parallel Program Design*. Addison-Wesley, Reading, MA, 1988.

218

[Coh88]   N.H. Cohen. *Ada as a Second Language*. McGraw-Hill, New York, 1988.

[CS87]   D. Cornhill and L. Sha. Priority inversion in Ada. *Ada Letters*, VII(7): 30–2, 1987.

[Dei85]   H. M. Deitel. *An Introduction to Operating Systems*. Addison-Wesley, Reading, MA, 1985.

[Dij68]   E.W. Dijkstra. Co-operating sequential processes. In F. Genuys (ed.) *Programming Languages*, Academic Press, New York, 1968.

[Dij71]   E.W. Dijkstra. Hierarchial ordering of sequential processes. *Acta Informatica*, 1(2): 115–38, 1971.

[DLM78]   E.W. Dijkstra, L. Lamport, A.J. Martin, C.S. Scholten, and E.F.M. Steffens. On-the-fly garbage collection: an exercise in cooperation. *Commun. ACM*, 21(11): 966–75, 1978.

[DS80]   E.W. Dijkstra and C.S. Scholten. Termination detection for diffusing computations. *Information Processing Letters*, 11(1): 1–4, 1980.

[DOD83]   US Department of Defense. *The Ada Programming Language*. US Government Printing Office, Washington, DC, 1983.

[For88]   R. Ford. Concurrent algorithms for real-time memory management. *IEEE Software*, 5(5): 10–23, 1988.

[Fra86]   N. Francez. *Fairness*. Springer Verlag, New York, 1986.

[Gel85]   D. Gelernter. Generative communication in Linda. *ACM Trans. Program. Lang. and Syst.*, 7(1): 80–112, 1985.

[Gri81]   D. Gries. *The Science of Programming*. Springer Verlag, New York, 1981.

[GS84]   D. Gifford and A. Spector. The TWA reservation system. *Commun. ACM*, 27(7): 650–65, 1984.

[Hoa74]   C.A.R. Hoare. Monitors: an operating system structuring concept. *Commun. ACM*, 17(10): 549–57, 1974.

[Hoa78]   C.A.R. Hoare. Communicating sequential processes. *Commun. ACM*, 21(8): 666–77, 1978.

[Hoa85]   C.A.R. Hoare. *Communicating Sequential Processes*. Prentice Hall International, Hemel Hempstead, 1985.

[How76]   J.H. Howard. Proving monitors. *Commun. ACM*, 19(5): 273–9, 1976.

[In85]   Inmos Limited. *Transputer Reference Manual*. Prentice Hall International, Hemel Hempstead, 1985.

[In88]   Inmos Limited. *occam 2 Reference Manual*. Prentice Hall International, Hemel Hempstead, 1988.

[JG88]   G. Jones and M. Goldsmith. *Programming in occam 2*. Prentice Hall International, Hemel Hempstead, 1988.

[Lam74]   L. Lamport. A new solution of Dijkstra's concurrent programming problem. *Commun. ACM*, 17(8): 453–5, 1974.

[Lam86]   L. Lamport. The mutual exclusion problem. I-II. *Journal ACM*, 33(2): 313–48, 1986.

[Lam87]   L. Lamport. A fast mutual exclusion algorithm. *ACM Transactions on Computer Systems*, 5(1): 1–11, 1987.

[LL73]   C.L. Liu and J.W. Layland. Scheduling algorithms for multiprogamming in a hard-real-time environment. *Journal ACM*, 20(1): 46–61, 1973.

[LSP82]   L. Lamport, R. Shostak, and M. Pease. The Byzantine generals problem. *ACM Trans. Program. Lang. and Syst.*, 4(3): 382–401, 1982.

[Mac80]   L. MacLaren. Evolving toward Ada in real time systems. *SIGPLAN Notices*, 15(11): 146–55, 1980.

[MC82]   J. Misra and K.M. Chandy. Terminating detection of diffusing computations in Communicating Sequential Processes. *ACM Trans. Program. Lang. and Syst.*, 4(1): 37–43, 1982.

[MP81]   Z. Manna and A. Pnueli. Verification of concurrent programs: the temporal framework. In R.S. Boyer and J.S. Moore (eds) *The Correctness Problem in Computer Science*. Academic Press, London, 1981.

[OG76]   S. Owicki and D. Gries. Verifying properties of parallel programs: an axiomatic approach. *Commun. ACM*, 19(5): 279–85, 1976.

[Pet81]   G.L. Peterson. Myths about the mutual exclusion problem. *Information Processing Letters*, 12(3): 115–6, 1981.

[Pet83]   G.L. Peterson. A new solution to Lamport's concurrent programming problem using small shared variables. *ACM Trans. Program. Lang. and Syst.*, 5(1): 56–65, 1983.

[PM87]   D. Pountain and D. May. *A Tutorial Introduction to occam Programming*. McGraw-Hill, New York, 1987.

[Pra86]   D.K. Pradhan (ed.). *Fault-Tolerant Computing*. Prentice Hall, Englewood Cliffs, NJ, 1986.

[PS85]   J. Peterson and A. Silberschatz. *Operating Systems Concepts*. Addison-Wesley, Reading, MA, 1985.

[Qui87]   M. J. Quinn. *Designing Efficient Algorithms for Parallel Computers*. McGraw-Hill, New York, 1987.

[RA81]   G. Ricart and A. Agrawala. An optimal algorithm for mutual exclusion in computer networks. *Commun. ACM*, 24(1): 9–17, 1981.

[Ray86] M. Raynal. *Algorithms for Mutual Exclusion.* MIT Press, Cambridge MA, 1986.

[SG84] A. Spector and D. Gifford. The Space Shuttle primary computer system. *Commun. ACM*, 27(9): 874–900, 1984.

[Shr85] S.K. Shrivastava. *Reliable Computer Systems.* Springer Verlag, Berlin, 1985.

[Sta80] T.A. Standish. *Data Structure Technqiues.* Addison-Wesley, Reading, MA, 1980.

[Sta82] E.W. Stark. Semaphore primitives and starvation-free mutual exclusion. *Journal ACM*, 29(4): 1049–72, 1982.

[TCN84] M. Tedd, S. Crespi-Reghizzi, and A. Natali. *Ada for Multi-microprocessors.* Cambridge University Press, Cambridge, 1984.

[WWF87] D.A. Watt, B.A. Wichmann, and W. Findlay. *ADA: Language and Methodology.* Prentice Hall International, Hemel Hempstead, 1987.

Index